Praise for

BRAVE NEW YOU

"Cory Allen is the present and the future of the mindfulness and wellness world. Brave New You *is an accessible and approachable guide to radically transforming your life for the better. This is a must-read if you care about personal growth and being the best version of yourself."*

— **Yung Pueblo**, #1 *New York Times* best-selling author of *Lighter* and *The Way Forward*

"Brave New You *is full of insight and practical tools to help anyone tap into their intuitive voice, build self-trust, and create the life they want."*

— **Dr. Nicole LePera**, #1 *New York Times* best-selling author of *How to Do the Work* and *How to Be the Love You Seek*

"Prepare to take charge of your life as Cory Allen, a genuine and gifted thinker, masterfully guides you to elevate your life with confidence, purpose, and extraordinary results. In this compelling exploration of self-discovery, Cory provides the keys to shaping your destiny, unlocking untapped potential, and igniting lasting changes. Brave New You *is a must-read for those seeking transformation."*

— **Vex King**, #1 *Sunday Times* best-selling author of *Good Vibes, Good Life*

"If you're looking to reframe your thinking, deepen your self-trust, and explore a braver way of being, this book is for you."

— **Alexandra Elle**, *New York Times* best-selling author of *How We Heal*

BBBRAVEEEE
NNNNNEWW
YYYOUUUUU

ALSO BY CORY ALLEN

Now Is the Way

BRAVE NEW YOU

A ROAD MAP TO BELIEVING THAT MORE IS POSSIBLE

CORY ALLEN

HAY HOUSE LLC
Carlsbad, California • New York City
London • Sydney • New Delhi

Published in the United States by: Hay House LLC: www.hayhouse.com® ***Published in Australia by:*** Hay House Australia Publishing Pty Ltd: www.hayhouse.com.au • ***Published in the United Kingdom by:*** Hay House UK Ltd: www.hayhouse.co.uk • ***Published in India by:*** Hay House Publishers (India) Pvt Ltd: www.hayhouse.co.in

Front cover design: Faceout Studios • *Interior design:* Nick C. Welch

The author of this book does not dispense medical advice or prescribe the use of any technique as a form of treatment for physical, emotional, or medical problems without the advice of a physician, either directly or indirectly. The intent of the author is only to offer information of a general nature to help you in your quest for emotional, physical, and spiritual well-being. In the event you use any of the information in this book for yourself, the author and the publisher assume no responsibility for your actions.

Cataloging-in-Publication Data is on file at the Library of Congress

Hardcover ISBN: 978-1-4019-7656-9
E-book ISBN: 978-1-4019-7657-6
Audiobook ISBN: 978-1-4019-7658-3

10 9 8 7 6 5 4 3 2 1
1st edition, June 2024

Printed in the United States of America

SUSTAINABLE FORESTRY INITIATIVE
Certified Chain of Custody
Promoting Sustainable Forestry
www.forests.org
SFI-01268
SFI label applies to the text stock

This product uses responsibly sourced papers and/or recycled materials. For more information, see www.hayhouse.com.

CONTENTS

PART I

CLEAR MIND, BRIGHT FUTURE

CHAPTER 1

MINDSETS ARE MAGIC

You're open-minded. I love that about you. You know how I know this? Because you just picked up a book written with the goal of making your life better. If you weren't open-minded, you wouldn't believe improving your life is possible. You'd keep living in the same patterns you have been. You'd accept that you're powerless. You'd believe your only choice is to keep letting life happen *to you*.

But that's not you. You're different. And what's amazing is that you're *already succeeding* at making your life better by reading this. Not because of anything you've read so far. Because by *choosing to take action* and seek strategies, insights, perspectives, and practices that will help you grow, you've proven to yourself that you *have power* and are in charge of your future.

Well done. You just placed yourself in a special group of people.

See, writing daily for an audience of over half a million people has shown me something remarkable. People who elevate their lives all have one thing in common. They believe that more is possible for them. That may seem simple to you because, as we know, deep down you already feel that. But it's worth noticing how profound it is. Being able to look at your life and see *opportunities* instead of *obstacles* is what makes magic come alive. And you've got it.

What's interesting is that even though most people can feel this is true deep in their core, they aren't sure how to make it real for themselves. They feel the energy inside of them but can't figure out *how* to start working toward a better life. Let me share with you how I know this is true.

About two years ago, it was business as usual. I was writing quotes to share with my Instagram audience. Without putting any extra thought into it, I posted what I'd written. It didn't feel like a big deal. I was just sending another idea out into the world that I felt was useful. But it *was* a big deal. In the blink of an eye the post blazed to over 100,000 likes. But it didn't stop there.

Every time I opened Instagram, my phone was churning away with notifications so hard I thought it was going to melt. Then 300,000 likes. Then half a million. I'd open the app, laugh, and just say, "Sure, why not" out loud. I'd be lying if I said it wasn't super exciting to watch this post ride a wave of epic virality. Then Erykah Badu commented on it, and I knew something bigger was happening. A few days later, that single post had over 950,000 likes, a quarter of a million shares, and had passed through more than *23 million* people's feeds. It's essentially like the entire country of Australia checked out my Instagram post that week.

Here was the thought I shared:

> Reframing your perspective is a powerful move. When you feel stuck or resistant, pause and look for the upside. Shifting your thinking from "I have to do this" to "I get to do this" engages curiosity. This turns every experience into a chance for growth, wisdom, and understanding.

The idea was something millions of people knew to be true, something *they could feel* but didn't know how to put into words and, therefore, couldn't put into action. Most of us know that how we think influences how we experience life. When we feel optimistic, the *world* feels optimistic. When we feel self-conscious, the *world* feels more critical. When we are in love, we see love everywhere. When we are low on cash, all we see are price tags.

What this means is that our negative views of ourselves and limited ideas about our future are just perspectives. They seem like they are true and "a part" of life. But they only seem that way because we've grown to accept those views as normal—and because that's how we think, the world reflects it back to us.

Here is the point of this book:

Just imagine if every part of your life that was creating tension, holding you back, and preventing you from *thriving* in the way you can picture in your mind was gone.

What would that look like?

How would that make you feel?

I hope you enjoyed that glimpse of goodness, because it's exactly where we are going.

This book will show you how to take your instinct that more is possible for you and make it a reality. Sure, most people know how they think influences how they live, but they don't know what to do with that information. They live passively and keep letting life happen *to them*.

> **This book is going to show you how to be *active* and make you happen to *life*. It's going to take you from *knowing* that more is possible to *living like* more is possible.**

You'll be guided by examples, stories, and actionable practices that you can immediately start using in your life. Within the first five minutes of reading this book, you'll start learning practical ways to take charge of your mind, let go of old thought habits, and approach your life with clarity. You'll quickly discover that doing this work is like knocking over the first domino in a long chain of positive events. That's because once you start reframing how you think of yourself, your whole world starts to change.

This book is a plan. It will start where you are today. It will guide you through everything you need to know to leave behind what's keeping you stuck and start living a life *that feels right to you*. You'll get there faster than you think too. See, I've been studying inner growth my entire life. I've meditated daily for 25 years. Over the past decade, I've talked to hundreds of the world's leading experts in psychology, philosophy, neuroscience, mindfulness, and personal development on my podcast. I've mentored people into making successful high-profile business deals and transformative spiritual breakthroughs. My online content has reached over a hundred million people.

I like getting right to the point. I want things to be concise, clear, and actionable. That's one of the reasons this book hits differently. I'm not going to sugarcoat things for you. I'm not going to pack fluff around ideas and drone on with weak stories to thicken up the page count. I'm going to give it to you straight. My heart raced many times while I was writing this book because I was so excited about what was coming through. I bet you'll know when you're reading one of those moments.

With that in mind, let's look at how the path of this book is going to unfold. So you know, the first part of the book is direct and brisk. I wrote it like that so we can cover a lot of ground in a short amount of time. As the book develops, the writing expands and softens as we go deeper and deeper into ideas until the end.

In the opening part of the book, we're going to do some mental housecleaning. You'll learn how to:

- Release mental stories that give you anxiety and make you imagine negative outcomes.
- Stop overthinking so you can make clear, stress-free, and authentic decisions.
- Control your impulsive thoughts so what you say and do are in alignment with your goals.
- Use free-writing practices to connect with yourself and gain power over your thoughts.
- Break the habit of creating negative self-fulfilling prophecies.
- Free yourself from feeling imposter syndrome so you can live boldly and with confidence.
- Embrace your quirks so that what's unique about you becomes your strength.

- Let go of self-consciousness so that you can feel grounded in who you are.
- Manage your reactions so you can live in the present, instead of staying stuck in the past.

The second part of the book is all about you. It's about prioritizing yourself and making sure that you're living life for *you* instead of simply trying to meet the standards of others. In this section of the book, you'll learn how to:

- Stop feeling guilty and start focusing on what matters *to you.*
- Build meaning in your life by doing more of what makes you feel alive.
- Create your own vision of happiness instead of trying to replicate the happiness of others.
- Identify and let go of relationships that aren't helping you thrive.
- Make yourself heard and felt by speaking from the core of your body.
- Mindfully communicate in a way that strengthens your personal connections.

Next, you'll learn how to start making the positive changes in your life that you've been thinking about. The third part of the book will teach you:

- Why you shouldn't settle for anything less than what you deserve.
- That you have the power to change *any* aspect of your life, even if it doesn't seem so.
- A variety of ways to take action and start making meaningful changes.
- How to turn your existing bad habits into new positive ones.

- Methods that will help you stay consistent and continue growing over time.
- Systems you can use to make your personal goals clear, so you always have direction.

Taking care of yourself is one of the most important and often overlooked aspects of living. In Part IV, you'll be shown how to:

- Learn to accept your own love, care, and admiration.
- Give yourself what you need, so you can always show up as your best self.
- Recharge with deep practices for physical and mental relaxation.
- Shorten the amount of time you hang on to anxiety and tension when they strike.
- Release resentment or judgments that are weighing you down.

Finally, in the last section of the book, you'll connect deeply with your intuition so you can move into your future with unshakable self-trust. You'll learn how to:

- Embrace the fact that you are allowed to redefine yourself as often as you want.
- Recognize and take advantage of opportunities that appear in your life.
- See that your biggest wins will turn out to be the last thing you expected them to be.
- Slow down and clearly hear the guidance of your intuitive inner voice.
- Trust yourself in any situation and make strong choices that serve you.
- Watch for the magic that flows through everything and use it to raise up your life.

Remember, reframing your perspective is a powerful move. Your mind influences how you see the world and yourself. So when you shift your outlook to one where *you* are in control, feeling confident, thinking positively, and acting with clarity, the whole landscape of your life starts to look different. Shifting your thinking habits will improve your quality of life and *make you feel more alive.* Getting a taste of the fact that there is something new, something fresh, and something bigger out there in life increases your hunger for what's possible. That hunger will naturally lead you on a path of personal revolution. When you *believe* you are capable, you stop shortchanging yourself, get clear on your goals, and make massive moves in creating the future you want.

I'm incredibly grateful to share with you everything that has helped me transform my life. I often reflect on what my perspective was like years ago before I started writing, mentoring, and speaking about this inner work. I remember back to when I truly believed that all my negative thoughts defined who I was, that my mental tension was "a part of me," and that redefining the future may have been possible for others, but it certainly wasn't possible for me. I reflect on that outlook because it keeps me inspired. Contrasting it with how I feel today is mind-blowing. It feels like two different lives.

Before the work feels like one reality, and after the work feels like another. Going through that growth process convinced me that reincarnation is real—but it happens in our single lifetime. Each day when we wake up, we are reborn and get a fresh chance to be more of who we want to be. All we have to do is choose to live as if that is true.

CHAPTER 2

OVERCOMING MENTAL STORIES

Clarity is realizing your mind is full of assumptions. Once you start watching your mind and noticing how often it fills in the gaps in your thinking, it will, well, blow your mind. Breaking this thinking habit will do incredible things for your happiness, peacefulness, and mental clarity. That's because our assumptions cause problems in almost every aspect of our lives. Later on in this chapter, we'll get specific about where we make assumptions and how to break the habits. For now, I want us to start with an overview of the "big problem" that our assumptions cause.

Making assumptions makes us forget that there are other ways of thinking. What this means is that as the patterns of our lives become well-worn, we tend to forget that *more is possible.* The groove of our experience, thinking habits, and beliefs about ourselves takes on the appearance of the ordinary. The more we continue in our behavior patterns, the more we get used to "how things are," and the more numb we get to the idea that we're capable of anything beyond that.

Assuming that where you're at in life right now is all that's possible does a huge disservice to your future self. It keeps you in a locked way of thinking

> **and limits your ability to break out of the story of who you have been so you can become the person you hope to be.**

Bertrand Russell, the brilliant polymath, shared good insights on this in his book *The Conquest of Happiness*. What's wild is that book was published in 1930, almost a hundred years before *this* writing, and still holds up. It's what I consider to be one of the first modern self-help books. He covers lots of great territory, but one of the things he mentions that has always stuck with me is the importance of cultivating an "appetite for possible things." Bertrand uses the term *zest* to describe this feeling that inspires us to believe we can always improve ourselves and our lives, leading to exponentially increasing levels of happiness.

Zest is that buzz we get, that feeling of magic in our chest that makes us dare to believe in ourselves. *Believing* in that feeling when it arises is how we break through what we perceive as the limits of our lives. What's curious is that breaking through once is all it takes. Waking up the numb parts of your life, taking charge, and *believing* that more is possible is how you ride the buzz of zest into a higher level of experience. After you do it once, you know it's reachable. Knowing that stokes your hunger and gives you an appetite for possible things. Then, you have the confidence to keep going, keep growing, and find greater self-belief, meaning, and happiness.

You may wonder what's holding you back from putting the idea that more is possible for you into action. I'll tell you: It's your assumption that you don't know how. For real. You can turn your life around with that simple mindset shift. Now, it may not be easy, but it is simple. You have to *choose* to stop believing that you're destined to live in the same patterns, attached to the same idea of who you are or who you have to be.

You have to think to yourself: "You know what? I have just gotten *used* to the patterns I'm thinking and living in. But they aren't all that's possible. I have the power to *choose* to believe in myself and focus on what is meaningful to me instead of what seems meaningful to others. I'm going to stop assuming this is all that's available in life, *start believing,* open my mind, and *make more of what's good* available for myself."

After that, you have to start taking action while embodying that belief. When you move through life with this mindset, bit by bit, you will start proving to yourself that higher levels are reachable for you—because you have started reaching for them.

> **One day, it will hit you that you have a real hunger for improving your life because you've finally figured out how to eat well.**

Assumptions Trap You in the Past

At the top of this chapter, we touched on the idea that our assumptions keep us trapped in the past. Here, we're going to go deeper into that idea so we can understand how it happens, what problems it causes, and how to stop it.

It's natural for us to settle into the same patterns of living over longer periods of time. Behavior patterns keep us from having to make too many decisions, which brings us a feeling of ease and comfort. After a while, we start living on autopilot. We coast through our days without a hand on the controls and stop questioning *why* we behave as we do. What happens next is tricky, and it's why many of us feel stuck.

> **We live in the same patterns, with the same thinking habits and the same outlook, for so long that it gradually starts to feel like that's all there is. We then**

> **begin confusing what we thought was true at *one point in time* with what is true *today*.**

Let me break that down a little more. Once we live in the same thinking patterns long enough, we forget that how we think isn't factual. And forgetting this means that how we think about ourselves can't evolve. Our sense of personal value, potential, or identity starts to feel unchangeable. That means that the outlook you had on yourself, your life, and your potential five years ago still feels true, even though so much has changed for you. Your assumption that "this is just the way things are" keeps you attached to old ways of thinking about yourself, which makes it impossible for you to let go of the past and embrace who you are in the present.

It's important to reflect on *why* you think and live in the patterns you do. If you don't reflect, it makes it too easy for your outlook to become outdated. When that happens, you start agreeing with yourself that "that's the way I am," and you can't improve your life.

Listen to What You Feel

Living with more intention and paying attention to what you're doing and saying while you do it is a great way to tell if you're living in old patterns of the past. The more you practice paying attention to what you feel in the present moment, the more you'll be able to hear subconscious signals that your actions might be out of alignment with who you are today.

How can you know which thinking habits are holding you back?

Your internal awareness is always speaking to you. Start paying attention to how your feelings resonate while speaking, talking, or thinking. When your awareness signals that something you're doing or saying doesn't align with who you want to be, listen.

You'll feel an internal tug, resistance, or dissonance. This feeling is there for a reason.

Give that signal space, patience, and attention.

There is *information* in our *sensations.*

Feel into what is arising. Practice self-inquiry.

Ask yourself:

- Does something about this behavior feel off on a gut level?
- Do I have to force this behavior instead of letting it flow?
- Do I know this behavior isn't for me, but I don't want to acknowledge it?
- Am I upholding this behavior to meet the expectations of others?

It's good if these questions stir something in you. It means you're starting to break the mold of a behavior pattern you no longer want to hold by shining the light of your attention on it.

Awareness is the first step of growth.

Taking the time to slow down and ask yourself questions like these is essential. Noticing your patterns, mainly which ones are serving you and which aren't, is the only way to make changes within yourself. Staying open, curious, and mindful is the best way to live in tune with who you are in the present. Doing this allows you to look inward, become aware of the behaviors you want to let go of, and build habits that improve your life, inside and out.

Your Attention Heals Your Habits

You'll discover that the more you practice being aware of your thinking habits, the more they will start healing themselves on their own. Once you become aware of a negative behavior you want to change, your awareness can't resist focusing on it. Your mind will start making a mental note each time it notices the pattern playing out. It's like when you have a sore tooth. Every time it pings with pain, your tongue can't help but touch it. Awareness of your negative habits works in the same way. Once you highlight behavior causing tension, you will become increasingly aware of it in the present moment.

How the Process Plays Out

After you notice yourself repeating a behavior that doesn't feel good, it will start appearing on the radar of your awareness as it's happening. Eventually, another part of your mind will start trying to intervene and shift that behavior in real time. Once you experience this a few times and become familiar with the flow, you'll be able to mindfully disrupt the habit and prevent it from taking place.

At first, you'll notice the old behavior *after* it has already turned into action. Then, you'll start noticing the action *as* it's happening. After more repetition, you'll become aware of the action *as it's arising as an impulse,* which gives you an opportunity to shift your behavior before it even starts.

This is a breakthrough.

> **Once you start noticing the impulse of the behavior as it rises in your mind, it means you have cleared extra mental space. That space is where you have the freedom to choose to act differently than your habit is urging you to. In that moment, you shift from being a *mind running a program to a mind writing a program.***

Your Mind Makes Assumptions about Everything

Our minds love nothing more than creating stories. An insatiable part of our brain called the *hippocampus* does this by sticking together distant, often random bits of information. Then these threads of story weave into larger stories about what's happening. Narratives like these are our minds' attempts to fill in gaps about the unknown. Even though these assumptions are trying to help us out by preparing us for what's next, they can create a lot of anxiety and lead us in the wrong direction.

Since these false stories appear in our minds, they *feel* true. That means that when we're emotional or fatigued, these narratives create *genuine tension, fear, or anger.* For example, we could begin to imagine someone we care about will be in a car accident while driving to meet us. Even though we have no valid reason to think this is true, once the story arises it feels like it's an actual possibility.

When we think something like this and our emotions start swirling, we forget that we aren't basing our worry on any factual information. For whatever reason, we had a story come up in our mind, we got sucked into our mental drama, and now we're reacting with real emotions.

How to Overcome Mental Narratives

When you notice that a negative mental narrative is spinning in your mind, the first thing to do is to take a beat, slow down, and *recognize the story as a story.* Reminding yourself that what you're imagining is just in your imagination will break the story's power over you. You'll still feel emotionally heavy, but the delusion that what you assumed is real will be gone. This is an important distinction because it allows you to get out of the mental loop of the story and keeps it from making you suffer more and more.

After you've reset your perspective, take calm breaths and once again remind yourself that the story in your mind is just a story. Then take big, deep breaths and imagine that you are blowing the tension in your body out of your mouth every time you exhale. Repeat this practice until you feel calm, centered, and grounded in the present moment.

Assumptions about Other People

Let's be real. We are social animals. And we spend a ton of our mental energy calculating the human game. Mental stories about other people pop up in our heads all the time without us even trying. Out of the blue, we'll start thinking about someone else's emotions, thoughts, or intentions. Of course, these are only guesses based on our imagination, but they really impact us.

Our subconscious fears love to manifest in this way. Sometimes our insecurities, desires, or anxieties take hold, and we start imagining all sorts of wild timelines and how people we know are acting in them. This is not good. Since we believe our mental stories are facts, we often assume our imagination is true and start treating other people accordingly. This is harmful to other people and our relationships and simply isn't fair.

How You Can Work with Mental Narratives about Others

When you start dreaming up a mental story about someone else, and it's causing you emotional distress, you'll want to handle it as we did earlier in the chapter.

Slow down. Don't react. *Recognize the story as a story.*

Take calm breaths. Remember that your emotions are a response to an assumption, not reality.

Once you have centered yourself and feel balanced, ask yourself if what you imagined needs to be addressed. Do you need to talk your feelings out with the person involved because you think there could be some truth to your assumption? If so, thoughtful and calm communication is key.

For example, imagine your partner arrives home from work and is short-tempered and distant. You might take that personally and follow the false narrative that they are angry with you and are being unfairly aggressive without addressing the issue. Being treated poorly can make you feel anxious and angry, changing your behavior toward your partner and increasing the chances of a conflict.

In this situation, it's wise to slow down, calm your emotional reaction, and recognize your assumptions about reality. After breaking the mental story, it's helpful to reset and engage with the situation with an open, curious, and compassionate mind.

Clarifying your perception is the only way to gain insight into the core of a situation like this. After resetting yourself, ask the other person to share their thoughts and feelings. In the current example, you would be patient and resist the urge to react and return fire toward your partner. Then, you would calmly communicate. Ask them how their day went, how they feel, and if they are okay.

A positive outcome could be that you discover your partner had a challenging day. They then go on to share that the only thing that got them through the day was thinking about being with you at home, feeling safe and calm. Your partner could then share that they need a few minutes to shake off the energy weighing on them and that they didn't intend to direct any of it toward you.

By being aware of your assumptions in situations like these, you avoid creating unnecessary conflict out of false stories. Practicing mindful communication like this is also a helpful reminder that the negative stories in your mind are just that—stories. After enough time, those reminders create an impact.

> **The next time you find yourself in the heat of the moment, getting worked up over your imagination, you can remind yourself to calm down, let go of the story, and reconnect with what's real in the present.**

Assumptions Steal from Your Future

So far, we've talked about making assumptions about others, ourselves, and the present. There's another area to cover that we make assumptions about—our future. Over and over, we make mental projections about what our future *should* be like. But almost always, things don't play out how we had imagined. When that happens, we get frustrated and feel let down.

Hold on a minute, though. Why would we expect everything we imagine to come into existence just as we want? We *know* that life doesn't work that way. Yet we still get bummed and frustrated when it happens.

This took me forever to figure out. You have to accept that creation is a collaborative process between you and reality. Allow yourself to be open-minded on your journey. Don't get stuck assuming things have to work out a certain way, then beat yourself up when they don't. Experiment, watch for unexpected doors to open, and improvise while listening to the guidance of your intuition. The most extraordinary things you will accomplish will come from unexpected places and be things you never anticipated.

Think big.

Watch for mysterious cosmic winks.

Redefine yourself and what you think is possible often.

Allow yourself to walk through the uncanny doors that open when you least expect it. Don't prevent yourself from thriving in the future because you're attached to a story from the past. The more you allow yourself to be present, unattached, and curious about the flow of your life, the more surprises will appear. This open approach to creating your path is highly fruitful because you're working *with* the flow of the universe rather than against it.

> **Life conspires to make your journey *more interesting than you can imagine.* It's why great things, when you think about them, don't just come from your imagination. They come from your ability to recognize the opportunities the universe offers you and be free enough from assumptions in that moment to accept the gifts.**

CHAPTER 3

YOU HAVE POWER OVER YOUR THOUGHTS

Swiss psychologist Carl Jung once offered that people don't have ideas; ideas have people. Turning this quote over in your mind is fun. In fact, watching your mind while you think about the quote will prove to you that it's true. Our thoughts have an interesting quality to them. They feel like they are happening apart from us in some way. Like when you think of something, it feels more like it "pops in your head" from the outside rather than emerging from within you. Essentially, I think that's what Jung meant. He was commenting that our ideas seem to come from nowhere, rent our minds like a roadside motel for an evening, then move on to their next destination.

Our relationship with our thoughts—as if they are from elsewhere—explains why our negative thinking habits have so much control over us. From a young age, we are trained to answer to authority. Parents lay out rules for how we should act in the world. If we don't follow the rules, we get punished. Teachers tell us what we should learn. If our interests don't agree with theirs, we don't get passing grades. Religions tell us what we should believe. If we don't subscribe to their spiritual script, we suffer supernatural threats.

For so much of our lives, people in positions of authority tell us what to do, how to think, and who to be. We've also been trained to expect consequences if we push back. And since we first heard those threats when we were children, a fear of rebelling against them lives deep in our core. So most of us keep our heads down, live inside the borders of what we've been told is acceptable, and try to get away with enjoying ourselves as much as we can.

As adults, we like to think we have a little more control of our lives and only have the boundaries of good decency and reasonable laws to stick to. That is not the case. We still live with our thoughts. You know, the ones that *have us* instead of us having them. Since our thoughts feel like they are from *somewhere else*, they take on this strange feeling of remote authority, which most of us feel compelled to follow.

Viewing our thoughts as this kind of parent-teacher-god authority figure and listening to them as truths we must follow is a thinking habit that wreaks much havoc on our peace and clarity. It keeps us from questioning what's arising in our minds; we just follow orders and act impulsively, and doing this turns self-limiting thoughts into realities. It makes us reactive, causing us to say things we don't mean and make snap decisions that don't serve us. It also causes us to lose trust in our intuition, which makes us suffer from overthinking.

Going forward in this chapter, we will change our employer/employee relationship with our thoughts. We will rebel against their authority, reclaim our power, and quiet the inner voice that tells us we can't, so we can hear the feeling in our heart that says we can.

Self-Limiting Thoughts

Strap in, because we're going to go way back in time to bust up our self-limiting thoughts. Like hundreds of thousands of years. As we humans evolved from a puddle of primordial snot soup to the hairy primitive ancestors we all know and love, we were fortunate to inherit many automatic features. Our hearts beat on their own, our breathing shifts when we need more oxygen, food turns into energy without our thinking about it, and so much more. What's interesting is that we usually only think about these involuntary functions existing in the body. Believe it or not, they exist in our minds too. Like our automatic physical behaviors, our mental ones are also designed to help us survive.

One of the ways that our minds try to protect us is by piecing together bits of information and projecting potential outcomes. For example, we could be walking along and see a tree falling a few feet before us. Our minds can keep us safe by projecting that that tree will smash us back to the Stone Age if we keep walking. If we are hiking and come across a raging river, the hesitation we feel is, again, our mind trying to protect us. The river *feels* dangerous. So our mind sends an intuitive signal to pause, proceed cautiously, or not move forward at all.

Self-limiting thoughts as we know them are this ancient process battling with the complex situations of modern existence. For example, being asked to speak in front of a group of people makes us feel fear. That is our instinctual self-protection mechanism trying to limit our actions to keep us safe. Our intuition senses that we'll be vulnerable in front of a large group of onlookers. So like the threat of the raging river, our mind instructs us to pause, feel our fear, and proceed with caution.

When you look to achieve a goal—whether it be personal, professional, or romantic—it's not uncommon for you to feel hesitant. The feeling of fear can arise, stopping you in your tracks. Sometimes your intuition softly speaks to you. You hear the thought that you should give up. Other times, your intuition reads that a high level of vulnerability is at play. So it meets that intensity level with equally intense thoughts. In those times, you hear thoughts that suggest you aren't good enough as a person, or worse, that you are worthless, powerless, or undesirable.

Something to understand is that your mind and body didn't evolve to make you feel good about yourself. Your mind and body evolved to help you survive. Your mind would much rather hit you with a negative thought that shuts you down than have you wander into a dangerous situation.

Your mind uses thoughts based on negative past experiences to limit your behavior when it thinks the time is right. For example, if you're thinking about asking someone on a date, you might feel real fear, even though there's no physical threat on the table. That fear comes from the fact that you're about to make yourself vulnerable. And your old-school animal mind doesn't like that. So it does what it can to talk you out of putting yourself in that situation. And it'll get the job done by any means necessary. Like sifting through painful memories of embarrassing moments and presenting them to you as negative thoughts. When it feels threatened, your mind will do anything and everything it can to give you a reason to finish your drink, go home, and avoid feeling vulnerable.

These thinking habits stall your growth, weigh you down, and keep you from living the life that you want. They are a voice in your head that would rather kill your dreams than make you feel unsafe. But the thing is, you shouldn't always aim to feel safe.

> **Safety is in the known. Growth, excitement, and the sensation of feeling alive exist outside of what you already know.**

Walk into the Unknown

Legendary musician David Bowie was famous for reinventing himself. Every few years throughout his career, he developed a new character, sound, and visual aesthetic. Bowie did this as a way to force growth and evolution. He refused to become stagnant. He was always looking ahead, willing to get lost so that he could find his way to something new.

In an interview, a journalist asked Bowie how he knew when he was making an artistic breakthrough. Bowie said it was a feeling he'd come to recognize. While working, he would feel like he had walked into the ocean far enough to be lifted by the water, only able to occasionally touch a foot to the ocean floor. The feeling that he was engulfed in the unknown, dancing with a force more powerful than him, was how he knew he was growing.

The heart of self-evolution is the feeling of excitement, fear, and embracing the unknown. You have to let yourself be vulnerable, not have it all figured out, and override the messages from your brain that say that you aren't capable. Flip your relationship with your self-limiting thoughts. When one appears, don't look at it as a stop sign. See it as a signpost that's pointing you in the right direction. Recognize that that feeling means you're on the brink of a breakthrough. It means you're about to encounter something new. You are about to stretch yourself. You are about to become something bigger than you had thought possible.

> **Understand that the thought that says you can't is an authority in your mind that only cares if you survive. *But survival is not enough.* It isn't all that you're capable of achieving. It isn't what you should settle for. You have more inside of you.**

You have the power to respect your self-limiting thought, set it aside, and walk into the ocean until your feet can barely touch the floor.

Overthinking

Imagine yourself as a child, standing in front of your parents. There's an intense energy in the room. Both of your parents are talking to you at the same time. One talks in a firm tone, demanding you go to your room because you've done something wrong. The other is talking in a warm and supportive way, urging you to go outside and play with the new toy they bought you as a reward for being good.

Of course, this is hypothetical. But picture what it would feel like if you were in this situation. You'd feel stuck and unable to make a decision. I mean, you've been taught your whole life that your parents are "right" and should always be listened to. So now there's no way to pick an answer. Either one is wrong because by choosing one, you'd be disrespecting the other.

Overthinking plays out in your mind in a similar way. However, in this case, the voices are your intellect and intuition. Both of these features of your mind have a certain authority to them. On a deep level, you can't disobey them. But they contradict each other. So you can't choose one to listen to. This creates an internal tension that makes you feel like you have pieces of paper being torn apart inside of you.

Overthinking is a form of resistance. When you're trying to make a decision about something, sometimes your intellect and intuition can get at odds with each other. The only way to keep from making the wrong move is to resist making a move altogether. Doing this allows you to get pulled further into the drama of your mind. Often, we don't fight this, as it is a way to validate stagnation. We also like to avoid making choices by overcomplicating the question and answer. If we can make things messy enough, we can agree with ourselves that choosing is too hard and go further into avoidance.

> **Overthinking makes us get in our own way. It's a thinking habit that keeps us from progressing in life because it tricks us into wasting so much energy that we get too tired to move forward. Don't waste energy fighting with yourself about questions to which you already know the answer.**

Your intellect is an incredible data-processing machine. That's why it's easy to confuse it with your inner compass. It's important to understand that your intellect is there to draw the map. Your heart and intuitive feelings are there to tell you where to go.

How to Stop Overthinking

Notice when you're overthinking. You will feel tight, heavy, and like you have two parents giving you conflicting orders inside your head. You'll feel overwhelmed. Your nerves will be frazzled. You'll feel stunned and unable to process information reasonably.

Practice *underthinking* when you notice you feel this way.

Slow down, relax the muscles in your body, and *stop* trying to figure out an answer.

Refocus your attention on what you're feeling rather than thinking.

What emotions or insights are rising from a gut level?

What *feels* right in your chest?

Can you let go of the direction you're trying to *force* yourself in so that you can feel where you're being *drawn*?

Create space inside of yourself. Remember not to try to pressure yourself for an answer. Let go. Doing this will bring your intellect and emotions back into balance. Allow the space inside of you to receive instead of take. Put your mind to work in service of your heart. Then just listen.

Impulsive Behavior

Taking power over our thoughts creates a spaciousness inside our minds that lets us be more intentional about our actions. This is good because how we act is who we are. We certainly don't want to let our impulses dictate who our future selves turn out to be, because that would result in a rather animalistic chaos.

Impulsive behavior often drives big and small parts of our lives without us realizing it. Especially when we get too excited or anxious. For example, being at a social gathering gets our nervous system buzzing. This stimulation raises our heart rate, makes our eyes dart around, and urges our minds to stay ready with witty comebacks. In the heat of the moment, we can make reactive remarks that aren't us at all. Then later, we wonder how it came out of us and never figure out why. While driving a car, a harmless error by another driver can make us blast off a kind of aggression that doesn't exist anywhere else in our lives. If we're in a tense conversation with our partner, we can snap back with cutting remarks that we'd never normally say.

Being caught off guard when something strikes a deep nerve will make you react impulsively. That reaction is an automated aggressive or defensive behavior. The behavior echoes how you attempted to *protect* yourself or *off-load* the intensity the first time you felt the specific emotional pain (likely during childhood), which is being reopened in that moment. For example, you may:

- Say harmful things when you feel threatened.
- Overperform your personality in groups because you are uncomfortable.
- Close off and shut down when emotional conversations arise.
- Smash something when you feel angry to displace physical sensations.
- Eat when you feel sad or lonely to fill an inner void.
- Scream when cut off in traffic because it triggers acute anxiety.
- Stay distant in relationships to protect yourself from the hurt of loss.

When you react instead of responding, it keeps you trapped in the past. That's because your reaction is your past programming controlling who you are in the present. Learning to diffuse this harmful thinking habit will bring much more peace, compassion, and connection into your life. It will also allow you to leave behind negative past experiences so that you can live with greater clarity in the present.

How to Retrain Impulsive Behavior

Start watching your mind. Learn to notice the feeling of electric intensity that rises in your body when your nerves are triggered. Then, be prepared to do the following:

- Take a breath before you speak. Doing this will give you time to consider what you will say before you say it. That time, even if only a few seconds, is incredibly valuable. It gives you the opportunity to choose a different way to proceed and break the momentum of your impulsive reaction.
- Pause before you take action. You can disrupt your physical impulses similarly to how you work with verbal ones. When you feel yourself reacting negatively to an emotional stimulus, stop everything. Turn to stone. This pause will allow you to *contemplate* and *shift* the behavior you are possessed to engage in.

> **Rewriting your conditioned reactions will free you from negative impulsive patterns that keep you stuck. A steady practice of self-awareness in peak moments will create sturdy mental clarity. With this vision, you will be able to navigate your path as who you are today instead of who you were in the past.**

Make the Invisible Visible

One of the tough things about challenging your thoughts is how convincing they can be. However, you can drain their mysterious power by getting them outside your head. Writing your thoughts down is an effective way to externalize them. It's great because it lets you see them from another point of view. Doing this has a powerful clarifying effect because it gives your abstract thoughts shape and shows them as they really are. It makes the invisible visible.

Whether on your computer, phone, or a notepad, try writing out thoughts or ideas causing tension. You'll find they are much less intimidating once you see them on paper. Thoughts influence our emotions. It can be tricky when we struggle with an idea because while we are thinking it through, we are also dealing with emotional heaviness. Doing this takes a lot of energy and makes it hard to think clearly.

Putting your thoughts on paper relieves intellectual and emotional juggling. It frees energy in your mind to freshly process what you're thinking. Looking at your thoughts on paper allows you to take on a third-party point of view. *You can look outward instead of inward.* Doing this enables you to look at the thought with less attachment and see it objectively and sensibly.

When you read your heavy thoughts on paper, you'll find that they are more manageable than they seemed in your mind. Seeing your thoughts this way gives you a chance to regain your power. You can then note anything you would like to work on going forward or release the thoughts as irrelevant mental noise.

Another helpful approach is to write down your challenging thoughts, then allow them to sit before reading them. *Doing this is always enlightening.* Experiment with different periods between writing and reading. Several hours provides enlightening results. Several days or weeks can be transformative. Giving your thoughts space before you read them exposes how impermanent and empty most of your thoughts are. When writing them, you are charged with a specific emotion and imputing a magnified degree of importance on what's in your mind. However, new thoughts, situations, and feelings wash through you as time passes. Your attention shifts, as does what seems relevant and essential.

> **When you return to read what once felt like the most crucial thing in the world, you'll find that those thoughts feel rather lifeless. Some of them might not even make sense anymore.**

At the least, none of them will have the tight grip on you they once had. Experiencing this is a good lesson for the future. It demonstrates that your thoughts *feel* powerful in the moment but are nothing more than noise passing across the stage of your mind. Understanding this takes away the authority your thoughts have over you and gives you back your power. It allows you to recognize them as chatter and keeps you from being bullied by them in the future.

A Note on Writing Out Your Thoughts

There is no right or wrong way to write out your thoughts.

Do what feels natural and *be fearless.*

One approach is writing down the exact thing you are thinking. In this way, you write a single sentence that defines or describes the thought you are having.

Another approach is free writing. Doing this is helpful if you have a hard time expressing what you're thinking or feel resistance when you go to write. Free writing is where you use no form, structure, or punctuation if you don't want to. In a radical, wild, and liberated way, you write down everything flowing through your mind. You don't even have to look at the page—place stream of consciousness on paper. Writing like this can be helpful because it acts as a mental detoxification. Returning to read what you wrote isn't always necessary. Sometimes getting it out is enough.

If you feel called to, you can go back and read your stream of thought. While looking at it from an outside perspective, you will be surprised to learn how the shape of your mind looks. You will see subconscious roots bursting through the surface and more meaningless noise than you ever thought possible.

CHAPTER 4

CREATING THE REALITY YOU WANT

Nothing makes us miserable and unable to feel bright and light quite like frustration, fear, and outrage. These emotions are some of the worst because they don't just pull us down. They actively eat away at our insides like they're trying to burn their way out. Anger-based emotions like these create a unique kind of tension in our bodies. Because when we are angry, our muscles contract like we're trying to set a powerlifting world record. When our body is tense, it makes our mind tense. And that makes our view of reality tense—which is exactly what we don't want.

Let's have fun and paint a picture with some metaphysical thinking for a minute. Consider the fact that our nervous systems extend throughout our bodies, starting in our brains and flowing down through our limbs like tons of tiny tree branches, all the way to our fingertips and toes. Our nervous system networks are strangled when we get frustrated and our bodies tense. This tension prevents energy and information from flowing through our bodies. That's why reaching a flow state is impossible while your body is full of tension. It just doesn't work. You've never seen a basketball player with a hot hand sinking threes all night tense and awkward with their shoulders up to their ears. Nah, they are loose like cooked pasta, flowing with time and space as if they are riding a cosmic wind that's blowing through the stadium.

Gaining mental abundance is an expansive process. It simply cannot happen if we are tight and collapsing in on ourselves. We have to be open, flowing, and feel like our bodies are expanding outward into space. When your body is full of tension, it makes it difficult for you to have clear thoughts, hear your intuition, and get into your next-level flow.

We want to reduce the stress we feel in our lives so we can spend more time feeling open and expansive. One of the leading culprits of tension is internal conflicts. These thoughts, projections, worries, and misperceptions make you feel stressed, incapable, and unmotivated.

Learning to recognize these thinking habits will help you work with them when they arise and release them. Doing so will keep you from experiencing inner tension that steals your energy and kills your inspiration. The beautiful part is that the longer you spend in your flow without fighting inner tension, the more positive momentum you gain. As an abundance of energy grows, you will start to live with more power, raising the limits of what you think is possible for you even higher.

Self-Fulfilling Prophecies

Everyone loves the idea that they can create the reality they desire. And for a good reason too. It's aspirational, attractive, and true. We really can do this. And I'm not talking about magical thinking or "manifesting." I'm talking about our incredible ability to visualize a goal, think our way through it, work hard, and bring that vision to life. What's talked about far less is the opposing truth.

> **People also have the power to create the reality that they *do not desire*. Understanding how we do this and how to avoid it is a crucial thought habit to learn. It will eliminate massive tension from your life and keep you from limiting your future possibilities.**

Prophecies are projections about what will happen in the future. Of course, not a single part of these stories is fact. They're all dreamed up in the imagination. Yet that doesn't stop them from feeling true to the person who imagined them. Fictional ideas about how the future will play out have a sticky quality to them. They draw us in and hook us. Not only are they fascinating to us because we are the lead actors in the role, but they are also often fueled by our anxieties, fears, and insecurities. Once again, our mind is trying to prepare us for what's next, so it searches its memory banks for the scariest things it can find to get our attention.

Before we go down the rabbit hole of self-fulfilling prophecies, let's think about this rationally for a moment. In theory, we should be able to use our mental projections about the future to calm ourselves, right? Wouldn't it be great if we could think through several potential outcomes, feel prepared, and then *relax*, knowing that we were more prepared? It would be great, and we can do this. But we have to learn to overcome the fear-based stories of our subconscious first because, let's face it, our worries are often way more powerful than our logic.

When we are swept away by the intense feelings of our mental projections, the chances are high that we will turn our mental story into a self-fulfilling prophecy. This is when what we imagine will happen *only happens because we made it a reality.*

Let's break this down and make it super clear:

- What we *think* influences how we *feel*. Whether the thoughts that come into our minds are reasonable and real or far out and false, they will still make us emotionally react.
- How we *feel* affects how we *act*. When emotion strikes us, it shifts how we approach the world in terms of our logic, patience, and intention.
- The way we *act* creates *who we are*. Regardless of how we think of ourselves, what really makes us who we are is what we do. We can have a huge range of negative and positive thoughts, but none of them mean anything unless we turn them into action. That's when they become real and reflect who we are.

With this in mind, a self-fulfilling prophecy is created when we allow ourselves to believe our false mental stories and then react *as if they are true*.

When we react to our imagination like this, it changes our actions, which affects reality, and *brings our projections to life*.

Examples of Self-Fulfilling Prophecies

I want you to clearly understand how this plays out in real life. It's incredibly common. Sometimes it happens in small ways, other times in large ones. Either way, it is a thinking habit that is responsible for a lot of suffering. Overcoming it will help you reclaim much peace and flow in your life.

Projection: You are anxious before you go to a party because you worry no one will talk to you. You fear standing alone and feeling awkward.

Made a Reality: When you arrive at the party, you shut down or overperform your personality because you're anxious. Doing this doesn't allow you to relax and be yourself. Because of this, people feel your inauthentic energy and choose to engage with you less.

Projection: You imagine you won't do well in an interview for an upcoming promotion because you don't think you're good enough for the job.

Made a Reality: You give a weak interview because you believe the story that you aren't good enough, and your confidence drops. Coming off unsure might raise questions from the interviewer, even though they initially chose to consider you for the position because they believed in you.

Projection: You have a history of not keeping up with good friends because you are worried that if you bother them too much, they won't want to spend time with you.

Made a Reality: Your friends look forward to spending time with you, but because you rarely reach out, they assume you don't want to see them, so they don't contact you to give you space. Then, the relationship drifts apart.

How to Prevent Self-Fulfilling Prophecies

The first step is noticing when you're creating a negative projection about the future. When you catch yourself dreaming up a scenario that isn't based on verifiable facts and feeling emotional about it, stop and label it as a false mental story. Then, remember the thoughts > feelings > actions model from above.

1. Define the specific thought. For example, you could say, "I think this meeting will be awkward."
2. Note how this thought is making you feel. For example, it could be, "This thought is making me feel anxious and full of tension."
3. Notice how that feeling is making you act. For example, you could think, "The feeling of tension is making me unsure of myself, tight, and unable to speak in a relaxed and open way."

The key is to *break the thought feedback loop.* Without defining your thoughts, feelings, and actions, you would likely believe the false story and proceed into the situation allowing your altered actions to confirm your projection. By specifying your thought > feeling > action flow, you can see it from a different perspective and step out of the behavioral pattern.

After you recognize the projection, exhale and release the tension of the emotions. Allow yourself to reset. Then shift your mental story from a negative one to a positive one. Visualize the best possible outcome of the situation you are projecting. Let that projection inform your emotions and fill you with excitement, optimism, and energy. Then, move into that situation *creating the reality you desire* rather than getting in your own way and creating one you don't.

Remember that self-fulfilling prophecies work in both ways. The difference is that the negative ones take shape on their own. We have to actively create positive ones. I know it's not fair, but it's how we are designed. As long as we know this, we can play along and beat the game maker at their own game.

Imposter Syndrome

Let's be real. We live in a materialistic culture that uses status, looks, and wealth to gauge worth. It doesn't matter who you are. It's impossible not to be influenced by this stuff. I mean, as much as I like to think that I'm pretty free from being attached to this kind of thing, I still check my Instagram analytics every day and look in awe when I see one of the many luxury supercars driving around Austin, where I live. Fact is, society trains us from a young age to compare ourselves to others based on what we have, who we are, or what we look like.

Getting a charge out of spotting a nice car or meeting someone famous is normal and harmless. However, constantly comparing ourselves to others is a negative thinking habit that causes major suffering. The truth is that basing our value on how we see others is a losing game. The levels never stop going up. Let's say you compare yourself to one person in particular, then work hard to exceed what you find valuable about them. Well, guess what?

You're not going to be satisfied. You're just going to look for someone new to put on your list of people to overcome. Doing this causes you to stay stuck in a never-ending cycle of desire, craving, and disappointment.

> **Getting into a cycle of comparing yourself to others creates self-doubt. Since the game is unwinnable, you'll never feel good enough. You'll always feel like you're falling behind instead of being proud, grateful, and inspired by how far you've come.**

A lifetime of society teaching us that we should base our value on others creates what is called *imposter syndrome*. You experience this when you feel like you aren't good enough to thrive at a particular professional, social, or romantic level. Even though the people you feel have more value than you are the ones who invited you into the fold, you still can't accept that you are equal to them. So this makes you feel like a fraud—like you've tricked people into believing that you have worth—and fear that at any moment others will find out how incapable you are.

Believing that you aren't good enough is painful and lonely. It's a thinking habit that limits your ability to thrive and deeply express how incredible and capable you truly are. Learning to break this thinking habit will help you give yourself the respect you deserve, feel comfortable around other high-performing people, and allow the best to come out of you wherever you are.

Putting Imposter Syndrome in Its Place

> **It took me forever to get comfortable with the fact that we're actually the ones in charge of deciding our value—not other people.**

Back in the day when I was a music producer, I started off being timid about how much I would charge. I was confident in my services, but I didn't believe I was worth that much. I ground out countless projects for low prices while trying to establish myself in the industry. I started getting solicited for bigger projects from people I didn't even know. They would offer me huge chunks of money to work on projects that were effortless for me. At first I would, believe it or not, tell them that I didn't charge that much, and I'd take a reduced rate.

One day, I got an e-mail from a guy whose Gmail avatar was him sitting on a Ferrari. He was offering me an exorbitant amount of cash for an audio composition commission. At first, I paused and questioned if taking more money than I would normally charge for that kind of project was ethical. Then it hit me that *many people in a row* had been offering me similar rates for similar projects. At that moment, I realized that it wasn't other people who were overvaluing my work. It was me *undervaluing* my work. I had imposter syndrome and didn't believe I was a person who could command that much cash for that little time. After a long road of battling with the idea of my own value, that insight helped me let go of my imposter syndrome and take charge of my worth.

What's real is that imposter syndrome is an illusion.

The self-doubt from imposter syndrome tricks you into feeling like you aren't good enough to be at a certain level. But the truth is that you really do belong there. People are not given promotions, offered projects, invited to join groups, or selected to speak in front of others for no reason. Opportunities like those are reserved for people with a proven track record of success.

Remember this when you start to feel like you don't belong in a group of people you see as more accomplished than you. Remember that no one gets invited to a higher level by accident. You made it there because you were so good in the first place. You're already thriving at the level. Now all you have to do is keep being you.

> **A secret from someone on the other side of imposter syndrome: Everyone is making it up as they go, even if it looks like they have a plan. No matter how together someone may seem, it is a guarantee that they feel like they are figuring it out in the moment, just like you.**

Imposter syndrome will deceive you into applying heroic virtues to regular people. Those you see as more accomplished than you will look effortless, wise, and untouchable. The truth is that they aren't. They are a person, the same as you.

Even when someone is successful, they still face constant uncertainty, fear of failure, and lapses in vision. The difference is that they face those obstacles instead of talking themselves out of trying. The sooner you accept this is true, the sooner you'll be able to stop second-guessing yourself, start trusting in your abilities, and flow into the future with self-belief.

Mindset is everything.

Consider this: if your self-doubt has enough power to shift how you see and present yourself to the world, the reverse is also possible.

When you feel self-doubt creeping in, *reverse your thinking.*

Replace *negative* thoughts with *positive* ones:

- **When you think:** "I don't belong here because I'm not good enough."

  Reframe: "I was invited here because I am great at what I do."

- **When you think:** "I won't sound smart while speaking in front of people."

  Reframe: "I was invited to speak because they recognized me for my skills."

- **When you think:** "I'm afraid of not being perfect because I'll look like a failure."

  Reframe: "I'm going to give this my best. It's okay if it isn't perfect. No one is."

- **When you think:** "I hope no one asks me a question I'm unprepared to answer."

  Reframe: "I'm going to bring my expertise to this. It's okay if someone asks a question I don't know how to answer. Not everyone can know everything, and it'd be great to deepen my knowledge."

- **When you think:** "I have to do this alone, or I'll look like I can't care for myself."

  Reframe: "No one can handle everything by themselves. If I ask for help, people will want to give me a hand because they care about me."

> **Don't give away your power. Stop waiting for others to permit you to level up your life, because it will never happen. No one will come along, tap you on the shoulder, and select you. You have to be the one to understand that value comes from the inside out. Set your worth high and stand by it.**

Know your value. Respect what you have to bring to the table. There is only one of you. You are a specialist. You are the only place the rest of the world can get what you have to offer. Act accordingly.

Forget about Being Normal

Feeling like we have to fit in is another thinking habit that creates inner tension and limits our ability to thrive and express our whole selves in the world. It's an empty gesture to try to fit in, because the truth is that there's nowhere to fit in to. This, of course, is why it causes so much suffering. Constantly looking to fit in when there is no place to fit in makes us feel like something is wrong with us and we don't belong.

Not true.

Let's think about this. Why would a person *want* to be normal?

To fit in?

To feel safe from ridicule?

To keep from being cast as an outsider?

To reduce the resistance we feel in society?

To fall in with others, so we don't have to find ourselves?

Looking closely at these motivations, you can see they all have one overarching goal: to be invisible.

Trying to be normal is a tactic. A cloaking device. A social strategy that allows us to hide in plain sight so that we don't have to face more profound challenges. While that seems appealing, becoming invisible creates the same problem we try to solve by being "normal" in the first place. We aim to be normal because we are trying to find our way. Instead of hacking through the untamed jungle of identity, we seek the path of least resistance. Using less effort is more leisurely. So we look at the paths that walked before us, blend them, set our course, and start living on autopilot.

Doing this leads to stunted growth, constipated potential, and a constant yearning for a life that's *more*. Following the blended paths of others *numbs our instincts* because it gets us out of the practice of listening to our inner compass. And our intuition is all that matters. If we want to feel potent, peaceful, clear-minded, and full of purpose, we have to be able to hear what matters to *us*, not other people.

Say Yes to Yourself

Ignoring your instincts leads to a life of second-guessing. Making it a habit to look around and see what others are doing before you make a move takes you further away from your true self. You can try to do what feels normal to be safe, but a time will come when that safety ceases to be a priority.

Walking the path of others will give you numb stability.

Embracing your own path will give you a life of meaning.

To keep growing, you must trust and listen to what feels right.

Crowdsourcing a path doesn't work.

> **Staying quiet and going along with what seems acceptable to everyone else's standards will leave you feeling far away from the real you that's inside, waiting to come out. You have to listen to what's pulling at you in the chest. When the universe offers you an exciting possibility, you must allow yourself to say yes.**

When you try to do this, there will be an instinct to doubt yourself, then find a reason why you must stay stuck in your way of doing things. That voice is animal-brain fear. It's the voice inside of you that's always trying to protect you. It'd prefer you stay coasting on a known and normal path than think big and bet it all on yourself. You will notice those moments when you get a blast of energy, and your mind is left pinging. Every cell in your body seems to turn on and point in a specific direction. *Those are important moments.* They are your past, present, and future colliding with the random chance of the universe, revealing the next step in your path. It is natural for a swell of energy like that to be overwhelming. The intensity of the feeling is why your mind tells you your enthusiasm isn't a good idea. Your mind is trying to calm you down and make you numb by disregarding the reason for your excitement.

Don't let the habit of wanting to stay normal limit your future potential. When your body lights up with inspiration like a divine bolt of lightning struck it, watch your mind. Notice that, in an instant, it will start discounting your surge of enthusiasm. When this happens, note the comments, then let them go. Understand them, then release them. If the voice in your head tells you that "You can't do this" or "You don't get to live a life this special, not *you*," remember that those are not facts. They are *self-limiting thoughts*. Note them, leave them behind.

Direct your attention back to the rising energetic feeling. Use that moment to go deep into your imagination. Visualize your success. Start seeing the steps that will get you there. Allow the excitement of the unknown and potential growth to give you the power to make it a reality.

Problems That Don't Exist

Finally, let's go hard against the compulsion to be normal one last time, so it's left broken in as many pieces as possible. Normal is an illusion. It's a mathematical average that doesn't exist in real life. If you mixed 10 of your favorite meals together, it would taste awful. Even though it is the average of 10 things you love, they are no longer special when combined. Normal is a concept—not a reality.

For this reason, it's essential to let go of the self-critical voice that shaves down who you are. These problems that don't exist hold you back. They make you numb to your dreams. The self-protective voices that try to keep you from following your intuition into the unknown will keep you from growing in the ways you already *feel* are possible.

> **The more you can live the life that feels right instead of the one you think is expected from you, the happier you'll be.**

Don't worry about fitting into the illusion of normal. Stop fearing your power. Focus on doing things your way. And let those challenges you spent time avoiding give you the meaning you've been searching for all along.

CHAPTER 5

CONQUERING SELF-CONSCIOUSNESS

We're all self-conscious to a degree. It's more than just annoying, unsettling, and anxiety-inducing. It's also part of our human nature. One of our species's greatest gifts is that we are aware of our awareness. It's also one of our greatest curses. Being self-aware allows us to create beautiful art, connect deeply with other people, and feel purpose in our lives. On the other hand, our self-awareness also makes us get in our own way, criticize ourselves, and act in reactive ways that have nothing to do with who we actually are.

If you experience those challenging things—and if you can read this, you're probably human, so you likely do—it's surprisingly *a good sign*. Feeling self-conscious means that you're a sensitive person. Being sensitive allows you to take in a ton of detail about your surroundings, thoughts, and emotions. Such a heightened sense of awareness gives you the power to deeply understand others, see the big picture, and express yourself in meaningful and profound ways.

You are burning bright.

Now, with great light comes great heat. What that means is that your awareness and sensitivity can get so intense sometimes that you can end up burning yourself on your own intensity. Learning how to work with your high-level awareness is an essential thinking habit to master. Otherwise, you'll spend a lot of time overthinking, double-thinking, and talking yourself out of following your intuition.

You experience self-consciousness because your strong sensitivity doesn't just amplify the pleasurable parts of reality that are easy on the heart. It also heightens your self-awareness of your negative thoughts and perceptions of the world.

> **Sensitivity is a gift. Know that. Even though the intensity of it can be hard to manage sometimes, no matter what you're dealing with in life, it's better to *know* than *not know*.**

Being overwhelmed by thoughts, emotions, and intense awareness can make you seek ways to numb yourself. I'll be the first to admit that I numb the intensity of my mind sometimes with a beverage or two. But it's important not to turn self-numbing into a habit you rely on. Otherwise, you'll start working against yourself, losing focus, and forgetting how useful your sensitivity is on a daily basis.

You don't need to numb your sensitivity or spend your life feeling overwhelmed by it. You simply need to harness it and make it work for you instead of against you. This can be done by learning to break specific negative thought habits, make your perspective big when it gets too lasered in, and use your inner world as a sanctuary when the outer world gets too loud.

As we move through the rest of this chapter, we'll look at several perspectives on self-consciousness, how to work with them when they arise, and ways you can start feeling more comfortable in your skin—today.

The Spotlight Effect

What's the root of our self-consciousness? Our ego. I'm not saying that if you are sensitive and experience self-consciousness, you're an egotistical person. I'm saying that our natural human design is egocentric by nature. That root part of us all—the foundation on which our minds are built—is responsible for the constant feeling that everyone is always watching us.

Our egos make us feel and *believe* that we are the center of the universe. Interestingly, even if we say that we don't feel that way, we are often lying, or at least not embracing the whole truth. I know many times throughout my spiritual meandering over the years, I've gotten to states of mind where I felt in my heart that I wasn't the center of the universe and that we were all one single beating organism floating in the middle of infinity. But if I stopped repeating the story I wanted to believe and listened to what I felt, it was always revealed that I was concerned more about myself than almost anyone else. Again, it's not even a bad thing. In fact, it's good to be that honest with yourself.

Curiously, we can't get around this feeling that we are the center of the universe because what *is* true is that we are the center of *our* universe. Everything we experience has to do directly with us *because we are the ones experiencing it.*

Stick with me for a minute, I'm going to get a little abstract, but I think it will help illustrate this idea with greater clarity. Our consciousness is like a camera. Everyone we talk to, everything we see, and every physical object we navigate directs its attention toward our camera's lens. That makes it *feel* like we are the center of attention. And why wouldn't we feel that way? We are designed to feel like we are the stars of the show, and that feeling is reinforced because, from our perspective, everything in life responds to us every moment of every day.

I probably don't need to tell you, but unless you're a social media influencer, feeling like you're the constant center of attention impacts your confidence in a negative way. It creates a false sense of how many people are watching you and judging your actions or appearance. Feeling this way isn't great. It applies a kind of psychic pressure to our beings that makes us tense, stressed, and unable to flow in the way we normally do.

Remember, sensitive people perceive more detail, which often makes them more naturally self-conscious. So if they are more sensitive, they don't just get stuck in their thoughts, notice more about any room they walk into, or focus more on their self-perceived flaws. It also means that they are more intensely aware of all the small egoic transactions that take place on a daily basis—like when you are in a room full of people, and you scan every person you pass with your mind, almost taking an energetic reading from them while trying to sense if they are doing the same thing to you. It's like a psychic handshake. And sometimes, sensitive people do hundreds of them a day.

These psychic handshakes are essentially noting the fact that *other people are aware* too. This awareness of other people's awareness creates what is known as the *spotlight effect.* Keeping track of how many other people or points of awareness are around you at any given moment creates a cognitive bias that makes you feel like other people are watching you more than they are. Or phrased differently, I should say that this bias makes you feel like other people are explicitly noticing *you* more than anyone else.

We've talked enough about what's up with self-consciousness.

Now, let's get to the fun part and start breaking its spell.

Sorry to bring up this memory, but think back to the last time you got a grim haircut. You know, one that you went into feeling like you were about to be deemed the freshest in the world and left feeling like you wanted to wear a cardboard box for a hat. When you stepped out of the barber or salon, you felt timid, deflated, and unable to take on the day with the same level of power you were planning on. Thankfully, I'm bald. But I remember those days of getting a bad haircut, and it's a terrible experience that brings up some deep feelings of self-consciousness.

Here's the mind-bender. Almost no one *you know* even notices when you get a haircut. And they certainly don't see it with the same level of detail and high standard of criticism as you. If they do notice, they probably don't really care or even think about it for more than a few seconds. If anything, they only bring it up because they feel obligated to tell you it looks good. Then, strangers, the people *who don't know you,* have no frame of reference for how you are "supposed" to look. So they can't even tell that you don't look "normal" because they don't know what your normal is.

> **The reality of self-consciousness is that it all exists in our minds. Most of the time, someone else couldn't even guess what you felt self-conscious about if you paid them. The things we feel that way about are so detailed, specific, and relevant only to our egos that they hardly matter.**

Another fascinating element of the spotlight effect is that it works both ways. The things we feel proud of go as unnoticed as what makes us embarrassed. When you say something clever or wear a pair of sneakers with an extra pop, they have less impact than we think. Most of the time, they go unnoticed. If they are noticed, they're just kind of noted as benign observations rather than indications of our mysterious genius.

How to Overcome the Spotlight Effect

Realizing just how shallowly other people comprehend what you say, do, and look like is wildly liberating. It gives you the space to let go, stop worrying so much about what other people think, and be as free and comfortable in your body as you can. When you start feeling self-conscious:

- Try flipping your perspective. Imagine how you would feel if someone else was feeling the same self-consciousness you are feeling.

  Do you care when your friend has a breakout on their face?

  No. You might notice it for a second, then forget about it.

Do you go into hardcore judgment mode when someone's clothes are wrinkled?

No. You might even see it and think it gives that person a cool artistic energy.

Do you write it down in your diary when someone makes a joke that doesn't land?

No. You hear it in the moment and forget about it a second later.

- Zoom out when you start feeling self-conscious. Minimize intense self-conscious moments by looking at the big picture. For example, say you're about to meet up with a group of people, and this will be the first time you'll meet many of them. In this situation, self-consciousness makes most people get weird, cling to the people they know, and not talk to the unknown people in the group. They do this because their sensitivity makes them close off inside to protect themselves, which dampens their good energy.

  When this happens, imagine you're looking at a group of people from an overhead camera view. Then, imagine the camera zooming out further and further. As it zooms out, you see people at the neighboring tables. Then you see the people in the entire building. Then you see all the people in the whole city.

  This exercise reveals how much is happening in the world at any given time. There are people around the world meeting each other and talking. Zooming out like this is a good reminder that the stakes are super low. You're just meeting a handful of the billions of people alive right now, passing through a moment in time that can never repeat itself. Everything is all good. Let go, enjoy your time, and embrace the moment like no one is watching. Because they aren't.

We Are All Background Characters

Feeling like we are the main character in a movie of life is another negative thinking habit that contributes to our self-consciousness. Again, this is a natural way for us to think. Our minds automatically create stories about what's happening in our lives to give our consciousness a sense of continuity and flow. This is a good thing. Life would be way too disorienting to function if our minds didn't work this way.

Let's have fun for a minute and play with this idea.

Think about what your life actually is. If you take a few steps back, you can see that it's just a series of individual events. One moment, you're a person sitting in your kitchen drinking coffee. Another moment, you're a person sitting at a desk in an office. Those two events happened in different places and times and have no connection to each other. That is to say, they don't rely on and aren't responsible for each other. However, your mind creates a story out of these two individual moments that gives you the feeling that "you woke up and went to work today."

Pretty cool to think about, isn't it? Our lives are slices of moments woven together by our minds to give a narrative flow to the stories of our lives. And what do all of these different stories have in common?

You.

Living in what feels like a long, perpetual story that only has to do with you makes you feel on a deep intuitive level that you are the main character of life. Feeling this way creates a lot of self-consciousness. I mean, we are the star of the movie. There's a lot of pressure to deliver. We often feel like everyone we know is thinking about us, even from a distance. Thinking this way makes it easy to get self-consumed and overwhelmed while managing a heavy load of thoughts.

There is something to consider that will help reduce the intensity of this feeling, but fair warning. It might not sound good on the surface.

> **The truth of the matter is that no one is thinking about you.**
>
> **Everyone is always busy thinking about themselves.**
>
> **And if someone does happen to be thinking about you, you're just playing a role in their story.**
>
> **They aren't thinking about you.**
>
> **They are thinking about how you relate to them.**

The fact that no one is thinking about you can feel like a bummer. But remember that *you* aren't thinking about anyone else either.

Main character syndrome is something that we all share. In truth, it is a logical fallacy. If everyone thinks they are the main character in life and only thinks about themselves, then no one is in the starring role. We are all background characters.

How great is that? It's super liberating to realize that everyone is naturally designed to be thinking about themselves all the time. That means that there's never any real reason to feel self-conscious. People aren't paying that close attention to you. They are paying attention to themselves. Keeping this in mind frees you up to get weird, enjoy the energy of wherever you are, and relax deep into the present moment.

Don't Change Your Behavior to Fit In

Of course, when we think of self-consciousness, we think about the anxiety it creates and how it destroys our flow and makes us get in our own way. But one of the biggest factors that usually goes unconsidered is how *exhausting* it is. The intense feeling of self-consciousness wears us down, which greatly impacts our thinking habits. When we're fatigued and going down a challenging road of thought, we become way more likely to think and react negatively, deepening our suffering.

How It Wears Us Down

Being in social situations where we feel like all eyes are on us tightens our muscles. Then, our mental and physical tension compounds and puts us into a hyperactive state of awareness. Our nervous system starts sizzling, we're filled with a silent panic, and we start overthinking.

Mental overdrive kicks in because in social situations we're trying to stay as aware as possible of as much as possible. We get into this state of thinking and feeling because we are trying to prepare ourselves for anything unexpected that might come our way. Feeling self-conscious makes us feel incredibly vulnerable. So we exhaust our minds trying to be prepared for any kind of conversation, comment, or negative moment.

Between our muscles getting tight and our minds being on overdrive, self-consciousness ravages our energy. It fatigues the whole system. Have you ever noticed that after you've been out for a while and have been feeling self-conscious, when you get home you're completely exhausted? That's why.

The Effects of Self-Consciousness Fatigue

> **One of the ways that we subconsciously deal with self-consciousness is by trying to disappear. On a deep level, we feel like if we make ourselves invisible, there is no one to be vulnerable, and therefore, no reason to continue holding the tension of self-consciousness.**

People are socially adaptable animals. We mimic each other all of the time without realizing it. So when we're feeling self-conscious, instead of wasting energy holding inner tension, sometimes we can become a blend of our surrounding personalities. When we do this, we adapt to the situation by staying quiet and echoing the leading points of view in the room.

To sharpen this example up a bit, think about how much nodding and smiling you've seen in your life. People do this so they will seem "agreeable," fade into the background, and become safeguarded from feeling vulnerable.

How Hiding Ourselves Prevents Growth

Blending in with the people around you when you feel uncomfortable weakens your connection to your inner voice. Even though doing this provides temporary relief, it keeps you from building the confidence that will help you overcome your self-consciousness once and for all.

Instead of shutting down and turning invisible when you feel self-conscious, seek genuine connections. As resistant as it may feel at first, push through that barrier and make yourself start or join an interesting conversation. Self-consciousness melts away when you start talking about something that makes you feel passionate. That's because part of your true self can come out and play. Talking about a topic you enjoy gives you comfort and automatically makes you feel confident because you have a grounded place to speak from. Doing this breaks the tension you're holding and lets you get back into your natural flow.

Take small steps to calm down, listen to your intuition, and trust yourself while feeling self-conscious. In time, doing this will make you feel comfortable wherever you are. Building self-comfort like this helps you anchor to your inner voice. The more you do this, the more you build a stable sense of self that's forever maturing into higher levels of confident authenticity.

The Only Person to Impress Is Yourself

> **Authentic confidence shows up when you stop trying to impress anyone other than yourself.**

Since self-consciousness leads to vulnerability, it will make you focus on what's important to others more than what's important to you. When your sensitivity is high, it turns you into a people pleaser. The idea is that if you please, agree, or look good to someone else, you'll be safe from judgment and won't feel the tension of self-consciousness.

Doing this is a survival tactic. Creating a character that you can play instead of following your instincts seems like a fair trade-off. For example, one might believe that being a diluted version of yourself might not feel great, but it's better than feeling the exhaustion of self-consciousness.

However, building a habit of feeling safe by seeking outside validation takes away your power. It puts you out of touch with your path and makes it impossible for you to feel self-confident because you aren't in the driver's seat of your own life. Living this way makes you simply react to what others find meaningful instead of staking claim and supporting what's meaningful to you.

Focus on Impressing Yourself

When you try to calm your inner tension by playing a role that you think is safe, you are trying to impress other people. Doing this is another method of becoming invisible.

> **Putting your energy into what seems to impress others is like running on a treadmill toward happiness. It will keep you in motion but never get you where you want to go.**

The way to release your self-consciousness and reclaim your power is to stop worrying about what others find impressive.

What makes you an impactful, potent, and confident leader? It's not showing that you can do what others have already done. It's finding something unique, important, and meaningful to you, something that may seem impossible to others, and then showing that you can make it a reality.

This may seem like a daunting task.

It's not.

All you have to do is focus on impressing *yourself* instead of impressing *others*.

Find what's exciting to you, what makes you feel alive and energized. For example, it could be going to the gym, becoming a better chef, playing an instrument, starting a business, learning to garden, writing a book, or recording a podcast. As long as it's a real passion that gives you an authentic energy buzz, it will work. Don't judge your interests. That's an integral part of not caring what other people find impressive. And don't let feeling self-conscious about what you love prevent you from enjoying what you love. What matters to you is what matters. Not what you think matters to others.

Now, spend your energy doing the thing that gives you life.

Make it a game.

Try to impress yourself.

Hold yourself accountable.

Get in competition with yourself.

Make sure you improve.

Do a little more each time. Learn something new. Gradually increase your ability. You will surprise yourself with how great you can become through dedicated practice.

Why Impressing Yourself Reduces Self-Consciousness

Focusing on what's meaningful to you and proving to yourself that you can get better at something that makes you happy is how you strengthen your self-confidence from the inside out. You build internal purpose, potency, and belief as you continue to impress yourself. Doing this makes the need to look to others for validation melt away.

Letting go of the desire to impress others puts you in a mental power position. When you no longer care what other people find valuable, there is an automatic internal shift toward peace. That's because the fuel for self-consciousness is a need to please others so you can feel safe and free from the fear of feeling vulnerable.

> **When you no longer care about pleasing other people or meeting their perceived standards, then the foundation of your self-consciousness dissolves. Feeling like this leaves you free to thrive in any situation. You feel grounded in your self-belief, comfortable with who you are, and strong with the knowledge that you can handle anything that comes your way.**

CHAPTER 6

BE QUICK TO SLOW DOWN YOUR REACTIONS

Even when we're lying around, doing nothing, staring into the infinite abyss of the ceiling, there's always this annoying urgency to be doing something. The feeling deep in the back of our minds is like an itch that we can't get to and scratch. It's also why the meditation app Calm was valued at $2 billion during its last round of funding.

Modern life has people stuck in the on position, and no matter what they do, most of them can't find a way to turn off. If we zoom out for a minute to look at our patterns, it's easy to see that we live in a constant state of *doing*. We have this deep feeling that there's never enough time or an end to the things we need to do. And if we try to resist it, we get to enjoy a nice blast of guilt that makes us feel like we're failing, which, once again, keeps us from releasing into the present moment.

> **Even when we are actively trying to relax, we are often still trying to "complete the task" of relaxing instead of just doing it.**

Let's take a moment to look inward and feel into this phenomenon. Ask yourself:

- How often can you focus for more than a few minutes?
- Is your form of self-care being on your phone or laptop?
- Do you find it hard to sit still without fidgeting?
- Do you feel guilty when you take time for yourself?
- How often do you forget what you are doing?

What's Responsible for This Feeling?

I wanted you to ask yourself those quick questions because sometimes our need to "do" can be so ingrained in us that we accept it as normal and can't see that it's there. Now let's look deeper to see where this need comes from.

For one thing, society grooms us to live in a state of *doing*. Everything we see—from marketing to social media to entertainment culture—pressures us to grind, hustle, and thirst for more. Culture teaches us that we are somehow failing if we aren't wealthy with high social status. Not only does this make us crave more "doing," but it makes us feel unwhole like we're missing something on a human level. The connectivity of technology has created social pressure making our e-mail, text, and DM response times so short that we always feel like we're on the clock.

Modern life is so full of information that we're *exhausted*. There are endless news stories, tragedies, diseases to fear, plotting politicians, account logins to remember, and social apps to refresh. The mental load crushes us as we try to keep up with the pace of everything around us. Most of us are too tired and overwhelmed to stop and think about why we are living in our patterns. We keep pushing forward and grinding ourselves down to keep the hamster wheel spinning.

Another more profound reason for our constant urgency is that we're aware of our mortality. Humans have the rare gift of being self-aware. We know that the longer we live, the faster time passes. This awareness makes us feel like a clock is always running out, whether we are 20 or 80. So we live with a constant tension that keeps us on edge. We think we can beat the passage of time by packing in as much as possible. But in a rush to "do more," we end up not being present for our experiences, invalidating why we are grinding away in the first place.

Why We React

Keeping up with the pace of the modern world is too much for humans to handle. We didn't evolve to have five e-mail accounts, three social media feeds, and 10 streaming services piped into our heads all day long. Humans are animals. Our minds are solid data-processing machines, but they are no match for computers and smartphones. Regardless, a wave of technology has swept us up, and we are all missing out on huge chunks of our lives by trying to stay on top of it all.

Your Brain Tries to Serve You

One of the brilliant features of our brains is that they are self-optimizing. They make it easier for us to do things we often do. They also pull our awareness away from stuff that doesn't matter to try and help us focus more intensely on what does. For example, say you have an analog clock in your room that makes a quiet ticking sound. It may catch your ear occasionally, and you'll notice it's there. However, that ticking sound will disappear if you focus on writing an e-mail. That's because your mind is shaving down the width of your perception and applying those extra focus resources toward what seems to matter in that moment.

Why the Brain Automates Actions

When our brain stops paying attention to the ticking clock in our room, it's trying to reduce our mental load. It does this so we have fewer decisions and less information to process. The goal is to help the *aware* part of our mind operate using as little energy as possible. This feature of the brain is more valuable than we realize. Imagine how overwhelming it would be if every sound, sight, smell, feeling on your skin, and thought were always in the forefront of your aware mind. Grappling with so much information would leave us slumped over, tripping out on sensory overload. That's why our brains put much of our behavior on autopilot. It keeps our mental hard drives from crashing.

Thankfully, when we are driving a car, we don't consciously think, "Right foot, pressing the gas pedal. Right hand gripping, elbow bending, wrist turning. Left hand resting. Right foot, lifting. Right foot, touching brake pedal. Left foot resting."

That would be far too intense. Instead, our minds shave down our awareness of those actions and *automate our reactions* to what's happening on the road while driving.

Reactions and Emotional Repression

Our brains create all these useful automatic behaviors so we can navigate the physical world without our heads popping. Interestingly, our brains do the same things while we are talking, listening to others, making decisions, feeling emotions, and thinking about our lives. Because our brains are such sticklers for saving energy, our minds often create these automatic reactions in response to *past negative experiences*.

Think about how exhausting it would be if we had to pause and go into deep personal psychological analysis every time someone said something that pinged our ego. Standing lifeless in the break room at work for four hours trying to shake off that time a kid in elementary school said your hair looked weird is not a very efficient way to live. So our brains keep us from doing an inward dive by programming an automatic response to those moments.

I know we're getting a bit deep here, so let's look at some examples of how this looks in daily life to make things clear.

If we feel disconnected from ourselves:

We speak without paying attention to what we are saying. Our brain reacts in social situations and tries to keep other people from connecting deeply with us, so we don't expose the fact that we're feeling disconnected from ourselves. This causes us to communicate with mindless filler instead of genuine conversation in an effort to create a barrier between us and the world.

When we feel anxious:

We might rush through everything as much as possible. This is us trying to "outrun" our anxiety. We try to overload ourselves with so many tasks that we can "blackout" our awareness and keep from feeling or thinking about anything below the surface level.

When our point of view is challenged:

We might react by shutting down our compassion and refusing to entertain any other possible perspectives. We do this because we feel vulnerable and fear that being wrong will make us look weak.

While communicating:

We might have selective hearing, talk over people, or make the conversation about us. Typically, we will react this way because our lack of self-confidence makes us need to try and appear dominant.

Being critical, gossiping, and judgmental in social settings:

Doing this is a reaction to feeling insecure and having low self-worth. We talk like this hoping that putting down others will make us seem higher in the social hierarchy by comparison.

When our emotions are down:

We often try to numb ourselves with excess food, substances, and entertainment. Doing this is an attempt to raise the dopamine levels in our brains while practicing emotional avoidance.

How Reacting Limits Our Growth

Mindless living is reacting to what you experience without considering your actions. Living like this has a significant impact on your ability to grow. When you're on autopilot, you can't make *intentional* choices. And if you can't make intentional choices, that means that reacting is stealing your ability to *choose who you want to be in each moment.* Allowing your reactions to take over simply plays negative behavior patterns on a loop, keeping you locked, almost possessed by the fallout from your past negative experiences.

Breaking the Cycle

> ***Mindful* living is sharing your attention between your thoughts and what's happening in front of you. Doing this allows you to pay attention to what you're experiencing and what you're thinking at the same time. This balance of awareness makes it possible to monitor your reactions, intervene, and choose to respond to the present in a thoughtful, connected way.**

Practicing this may sound difficult, like patting your stomach and rubbing your head at the same time. But I assure you, it's not only quite easy, it can become fascinating too. When you start paying attention to your mind, you'll start learning about yourself, gaining personal insights, and becoming able to fine-tune how you show up in the world.

Here's how noticing your reactions plays out in real life:

When you first start paying attention to your reactive behavior, you'll likely notice reactions *after* they happen. This may not sound like much, but it's great progress. You've become aware of the fact that you're reacting, and that's huge. You'll notice the *automated response* and feel a *muted negative emotion*. For example, a friend could comment on your new jacket, and because you feel a little vulnerable rocking a new style, you may make a sarcastic reactive comment. In this situation, you'd notice what you said after you said it and feel the negative emotional impact.

After you've spent time watching your mind and noticing when you react to a thing, you'll build the skill of *intervening in your reactions*. The mental space you've cultivated by being more self-aware gives you the opportunity to *choose* a new action in the moment rather than allow your *reaction* to play out. So you'll notice the *impulse* or the craving urge to say or do something and be able to change the course of that action before it comes alive.

Continuing with our above example, you might feel vulnerable about your new jacket. When your friend comments, you feel the negative emotion in your chest, your adrenaline kicks in, and the tense desire to react with a defensive comment appears. Instead of allowing your reaction to play out, you recognize what's happening, take a beat, and choose to *respond* in a kind way instead of reacting negatively. Doing this not only prevents pointless harm for you and others but also allows you to take back your power and choose to be a better, healed, and more confident version of yourself.

How to Prevent Reactions

1. Pause, slow down, and take a breath before speaking.

Mindlessly speaking to others is one of the most common forms of reaction. Words are more powerful than we realize, so this is a good one to work on. When we feel defensive, vulnerable, angry, or down, we react to those around us by snapping at them or being short. Most of the time, we aren't even thinking about what we're saying. We unfairly use our words to offload what we're feeling on others.

For example, if we're feeling frustrated and someone rubs us the wrong way, we might say something mean or aggressive to give them a taste of what we're feeling. Think of the last time you did this. Recall when you were overloaded with tension and blasted off at someone. It almost feels like there's a blank in your memory, doesn't it? Like you were hypnotized during those few seconds. That's the feeling of reaction.

When you notice you're not in a good headspace, it's wise to slow things down, pause, and take a breath before you speak. Doing this will lower your heartbeat and help you calm down and think more clearly. The few seconds of that breath puts a gap between your thinking and your actions. Doing this gives you the time to let go of your reactive energy, speak with clarity, and shift your behavior pattern into a constructive form of expression.

2. Take a moment to ground yourself when feeling anxious.

Whenever we feel anxious, our brain shifts into fight-or-flight mode. This shift alters how we perceive reality. The intensity level of everything increases. People's words hit us extra hard and feel threatening. Challenges seem unbeatable. Our attention becomes panicky and darts around, which makes it difficult to focus on one thing. Feeling anxious is a prime opportunity for reaction. That's because we are so overwhelmed by what we feel that almost all our actions go on autopilot. Acting from a fear-based mindset makes us say things to keep people away, look for unhealthy ways to numb ourselves, and make blurry decisions.

As you notice your anxiety increasing, use that feeling as a signal that it's time to take action. The sooner you sense your tension rising and counteract it, the better off you'll be. Think of anxiety like a fire. You can stomp out a few smoldering embers with your foot. However, a forest fire takes a whole crew to battle.

You can soothe your anxiety by taking 10 calm and slow breaths. If you can take even more breaths, that's wonderful. On each exhale, relax the muscles in your body as much as possible. Slowing your breathing sends signals to your mind that your body is safe. While feeling anxious and in fight-or-flight mode, the tension in your body makes your mind believe that your environment is physically dangerous. This perception creates a feedback loop between your body and mind, increasing your anxiety. Intervening by taking long and slow intentional breaths will break the cycle, tell your brain that you aren't in danger, and relieve the intensity of your anxiety.

3. Cultivate compassion by looking at different perspectives.

Our ego can feel threatened and react when challenged. We can act mindlessly when someone disagrees with us, doesn't show us the respect we believe we deserve, or doesn't validate the value we believe we're bringing to the table. Our ego is sensitive because it's the core of our being. When it feels provoked, it hits us on the deepest level, which often causes the harshest reactions. In an instant, we can become angry, judgmental, spiteful, and cold. Sensitive egos have a constant need to feel strong and in control. When there is a conflict with that feeling, the reaction is to cut off compassion, be aggressive, and regain a sense of power however possible.

Egoic reactions can get ugly fast. When you feel your ego challenged and negative emotions start to rise, it's wise to take a step back, withhold your actions, and consider the situation from multiple perspectives. In most cases, whoever challenged your ego didn't intend to do so. They likely stumbled upon one of your triggers without understanding how it would hit you. They probably aren't even aware that what they said was harmful to you. Instead of reacting by becoming aggressive and cold, entertain the possibility that the story you have in your mind about what happened isn't the whole story. Ask clarifying questions if you need more detail about what was said and why. Allow some compassion to flow in. Give yourself and others the benefit of the doubt. Be as empathetic with yourself as you would with a dear friend.

Owning Yourself in the Present

Thoughtfully responding to life instead of reacting to it is how to free yourself from mixed-up memories, bad imprints, and the limiting idea that who you once were is who you always have to be. Be gentle with yourself. It takes time and repetition to begin noticing your reactive behaviors and figure out the best way for you to intervene. There's lots of trial and error involved. But real, lasting change is possible. All you have to do is be patient, put in the work, and be assertive when necessary.

Another important thing to remember is not to expect perfection. We are prone to being far too hard on ourselves. After we become aware of something we want to change about ourselves, it's inevitable that we will slip up and react. That's no big deal. Many reactions have been with us for a long time. So they will take some time and repetition to change. Each time your reactions pop up and you change the course of your behavior, the automatic response will lighten up more and more until, one day, it virtually disappears.

It's not fair to expect that we'll ever be completely free of reactive behaviors. We're human, after all. We'll snap at our partners when we are tired or stressed. We'll get flustered in annoying traffic situations. We'll say something sharp when we're feeling a little edgy. What's important at a developed stage of awareness is that we take responsibility for our inevitable slipups as quickly as we can. Be accountable when you notice you've reacted negatively toward someone. Apologize. Learn from the mistake. Keep moving forward.

Perfection is not the goal. It's all about aiming to be better than you were yesterday. Working with your reactions and learning to consciously respond in the moment will open tremendous paths on your growth journey. That's because reactions are the old parts of you that no longer match who you are today.

> **By taking charge of your reactions, you are taking control of who you are. You are undoing the negative habits that are limiting your happiness. You are releasing the repressed emotions that have been lying dormant. You are claiming who you want to be in the present instead of being controlled by who you were in the past.**

PART II

SELF-HEALING IS SELF-DISCOVERY

CHAPTER 7

FOCUS ON WHAT MATTERS TO YOU

There's no "one size fits all" for personal evolution. We all come from unique backgrounds, have original ways of seeing the world, and, most importantly, have *different needs*. Once we start walking our path and doing inner work, we'll have an intuition as to where we need to put our energy and what we might do to improve our lives. Growth is an intensely individual pursuit in that no two paths look alike. However, if we're real about how inner transformation takes place, we'll see that we are greatly influenced by the people around us.

Seeking ways to self-heal is like dragging a net through the ocean. There are so many ways to approach our growth—and such a variety of effective methods—that we must search through many of them to find what works for us. We cast our net into the Internet, library, or podcast app and drag the digital waters hoping to find the insight or practice that unlocks something inside us. We also talk to our friends about their practices and sometimes follow along out of curiosity and trust.

Seeking is certainly a part of the growth process. Yet it's wise to pay attention to how the influence of others can keep us stuck trying to make the progress we want instead of the progress we need. Self-help culture is an alluring and influential force. As I'm sure you've seen, there's always a fresh wave of experts flowing across the social media, podcast, and YouTube landscape. Nothing against experts and people with large public profiles. They generally have useful and thought-provoking information to share. These influential people bubble up in society because what they offer resonates deeply with where culture is at that moment. But the thing about this is that you aren't culture. You are an individual within the culture. So what everyone else needs might not be what you need at that moment in time.

It's important to keep an eye on your relationship with self-help culture. Taking the help that culture is serving you instead of listening to your inner voice and finding the next important step can jam you up.

> **Someone will always be out there telling you what you need and what will improve your life. Yet, to make real growth, it's crucial to understand what you need in your life *at the moment* and act accordingly.**

Growth paths are nonlinear. We all need to address different parts of ourselves at different times. We'll suffer and waste time if we try to force ourselves to do otherwise. Buying a copy of *Atomic Habits* because it's tremendously popular isn't going to help you much if you need to learn how to create boundaries in unhealthy relationships.

To make matters even murkier, much of the information online about personal growth is chunked out to create easily digestible content. So it's all quick blasts of information that read like instant and definitive solutions. Seeing so much content like this on inner growth can create an illusion that leads to feelings of pressure and frustration. Seeing 10 ways to "optimize" your mental health and well-being everywhere you look is hard. It can make you feel lost and like you're falling behind when doing a few things from that list doesn't move the needle for you.

The truth is that you can follow the steps on every highly perfected two-minute YouTube wellness video, go on a keto diet, drink nothing but water, hit the sauna to activate your heat shock proteins and take cold plunges every morning, and it won't matter. Sure, doing some of those things might help you feel healthier. Still, they're addressing problems that other people are telling you that you need to fix rather than the ones that you feel pulling at you on the inside.

That's why self-help culture can leave people yearning to be well without ever helping them arrive where they hope to be. There's so much content out there telling us that this or that will solve our problems, make us happier, and change our lives. When we try some of those things out, we discover that we may have some surface-level improvements, but nothing has fundamentally changed. That is confusing because—hey—this video has three million views, and the person in it has crystal-clear eyes and razor-sharp cheekbones. And this other guy must know what protocol you need because he's a brawny professor. You might ask yourself why some of the stuff you see offered doesn't help you yet seems to help others. The problem is that if we seek change and only look at the options sold to many, we won't ever be able to find what we truly need for ourselves.

Self-Healing Is Self-Discovery

It's impressive when someone says they've been meditating for 20 years. We may wonder what their perspective is like, how their mind works, or how centered they feel. But one thing that we usually don't wonder is: Why are they still meditating? I mean, if they've been going for 20 years, you'd think they would have gotten there by now. The answer to this question is that our path is called a path for a reason. It's long and never-ending. That may sound daunting, like I've just given you an endless amount of homework. It's quite the opposite.

Personal transformation is an act of *self-discovery.* If you remember the earlier chapters in the book, awareness plays a huge role in our ability to grow. Really, it's the key that gets the whole party started.

> **If we don't know *why* we are suffering or what it is about ourselves that we want to change, then we'll never be able to get anywhere. To get in touch with the unknown parts of ourselves, we have to learn to live with a kind of open awareness. We have to gently watch our minds so that we can learn who we are and how we'd like to grow.**

Watching Your Mind

Watching your mind may sound strange. Don't worry, it's easy. In fact, it's so easy that you already do it sometimes. The key is doing it consciously and more regularly. Watching your mind is when you observe your flow of thoughts from a distance. You know that feeling you get when it's like there's a camera in the back of your brain pointing forward? When your awareness is wide and calm, and you can see what you're thinking and doing from a broader perspective? I'm sure you know that feeling. You probably slip into that mode of awareness when you're sitting around relaxing or doing a mindless task that's keeping your body busy. You may find this kind of meta-awareness turns on by itself is when you're going for a walk, doing the dishes, or folding laundry.

That level of awareness is appropriately called the *witness mind.* It means that you're simply *witnessing* what's happening in the present moment rather than being distracted by the drama of your thoughts and the performance of your identity. Developing a closer connection with this type of awareness is incredibly valuable. It's the foundation of mindfulness. Being aware of your thoughts as they're happening allows you to gain deeper insight into your feelings and increases your mental clarity. What's funny is that people usually assume "mental clarity" means that you aim to have a mind without thoughts. That's not true.

> **Mental clarity is having an *awareness* of what thoughts and impulses are arising in your mind so you can act with more self-aware intention rather than being blindsided by your conditioned reactivity.**

Let's do a quick experiment to help get in touch with our witness mind.

1. Close your eyes, relax your body, and take a few calm breaths.
2. Simply start noticing everything that you're aware of. Don't try to force anything. Allow whatever wants to come to your attention to do so. Open your senses.
3. Then, let it go and allow the next thing to arise.
4. Breathe calmly and gently. Imagine there's a camera in the back of your head aiming forward. Notice the fragments of thoughts appear and disappear.
5. Feel the muscles in your body that are sending you random signals. Hear the sounds in the space you're in.
6. Let it all flow by without trying to engage with it. Like you're sitting on the beach, watching the waves of the ocean crash.
7. Be a point of awareness that exists in the present moment.
8. Do nothing but watch it all happen.

Welcome back. I hope you enjoyed playing with your awareness, and now I'll tell you why I wanted us to do that experiment. Once you're aware of the witness mind, it has a real habit of sticking around. That's a good thing. When you're more aware of what's happening in your mind and less attached to the drama of it, you can go through life with the kind of "open awareness" that I mentioned earlier.

Remember: self-growth is self-discovery. By having an outside view of your thoughts, feelings, and actions, you can see yourself more objectively. That's valuable because it *increases your awareness*, which gives you greater personal insight and allows you to *discover* what's inside of you that you need to focus on. Being tuned in to your witness mind increases your awareness in the present moment, which helps you notice your behaviors, thoughts, and actions as they happen. That way, you can move through life with open awareness and notice in real time what you're doing and thinking that may be out of alignment with who you want to be. By noticing these small, nuanced things, you can home in on, clearly define, and consciously work through them by revising your behavior patterns.

After you've built this skill, you can use it forever. When you tune in to your witness mind and start watching your inner flow more consciously, it'll be easy to spot blatant things you'd like to improve. For example, you could notice that you talk down to yourself at key moments, slide into critical states of mind when you're tired, start people-pleasing when you're anxious, or get defensive when someone tries to give you personal feedback. Big behaviors like these are easy to spot because they are on the surface. After you've spent some time digging into your internal landscape, the refinements will become smaller and more nuanced. Then, you'll start noticing small things you'd like to shift. Like when you need to listen instead of talk, be mindful of other perspectives, or not get drawn into your own brief mental stories.

Going on this path of self-awareness is a beautiful gift because the more attachments you can let go of, the freer and more vibrant you'll feel. I can speak from experience. I've been working on my inner life for over 20 years. Every year, it's clear that I've left behind more thoughts and behaviors that make me unhappy and found my way to deeper insights and ways of being that cultivate a sense of peace, clarity, and awareness.

What's funny is that every year I feel like I'm just getting started. Each personal insight you have shows you something about yourself that you didn't know. Living in a constant flow of self-discovery means that you're living in a constant flow of self-transformation. The newness of discovery keeps you and the work feeling fresh. And it shows that there are more possibilities living inside of us than we can ever comprehend.

All of this is why focusing on what matters to you is so important. Self-help culture provides a ton of useful thoughts, tools, and perspectives that you can use when the time comes. And I'd say that it's valuable to keep soaking up those ideas, experimenting with them, and storing them away in the back of your mind. But they can't guide you to where you need to go inside of yourself. Only you can. You have to be patient, live with open awareness, watch what arises inside of you, and meet it in the present moment.

> **Once you learn to watch your mind, you'll never be without a teacher.**

Solving the Happiness Problem

We all want to be happy. However, the idea of happiness is so rich, complex, and relative that we can have a hard time defining what it means. If asked what happiness is, we might say something like being healthy, spending time with people we love, or making ends meet so we can enjoy ourselves. While those things are beautiful, they don't get at what we're thinking about when we wonder what it means to be existentially happy.

Interestingly, I think one of the issues with the idea of finding happiness is that it's presented in society as a form of personal wealth. And with the promise of abundance comes the fear of scarcity. We're told from early on that our goal in life is to be happy. Otherwise, we aren't making it, something is wrong with us, and our life isn't working out. So we go through life searching for what might make us happy. Because finding happiness is harder than it sounds, many people go for the default things everyone says are supposed to make us happy. Like getting a nice place to live, climbing the ladder at work, and building a little more personal status than the next person. Of course, these things don't guarantee happiness—they often induce greater stress—so when people achieve what are meant to be universal goals, they feel let down when those goals make them feel . . . nothing.

The idea that happiness is something we are supposed to "get" gives it a materialistic quality that makes it unreachable.

That's what gives it the same flavor as personal wealth. We're so conditioned that no matter how well we're doing financially, we always wish we were doing a little better. That perspective prevents us from enjoying and appreciating how well we *are* doing. The same goes for happiness. No matter how incredible our lives are, we always feel like we're missing something and should be a little happier. Again, this makes us miss much of the joy we experience every day because it pulls us out of a present-minded state of gratitude and into a state of desire.

I've thought about this a lot over the years. What I came away with is that our happiness problem comes from a poor definition rather than our ability to achieve it. Happiness isn't something you "get" or find your way to. It's a byproduct of something else.

The Happiness Afterglow

The broad and subjective definition of happiness is one of the main things that makes it elusive. So let's forget the current definitions and consider what we might *feel* if we were to get where we wanted to be. We would feel at ease, not hung up on small problems, satisfied, and good about what we've accomplished—all with an optimistic outlook on the future. If we were to look for another word that might fit a bit better for what I just described, we could come up with *fulfillment.*

Now we're talking. Feeling fulfilled is something that we can define, act on, and aim toward. That's a much nicer road ahead than the illusive and ever-changing notion of happiness. But that raises the next question. How do we feel fulfilled? By doing something that feels meaningful to us. Now, the interesting thing about meaning is that people overthink it to death. It doesn't have to be some lofty pursuit that contributes to your personal status. In fact, the opposite of that is best. That's because there is no meaning *in* life. We have to create it for ourselves.

I want to clear up any possible confusion real quick before we go on. People often confuse the idea of the meaning *in* life with the meaning *of* life. We're talking about meaning *in* life. The other one is easy. The meaning *of* life is to live. That's all there is to it. It's simple, always present, and never changes. However, meaning *in* life is a different story. We have to create meaning for ourselves. If we don't, then we won't have much. If you want to create meaning, the first step is not to overcomplicate it. The second is to be honest with yourself. And the third is not to worry about what others think is meaningful.

To create meaning, you must listen to your inner voice and pay attention to whatever you do that makes you feel a deep sense of connection, clarity, and goodness. As I said earlier, the less lofty and more straightforward, the better. Many people find meaning in gardening, playing an instrument, reading books, donating their time to charities, and so on. These are all good things, but what they are isn't what matters. It's how they make a person *feel.* To build meaning, you have to put energy into something that matters *to you.* That's the only way it works. Doing what seems to be meaningful to others doesn't. It has to come from the inside out.

Once you find something in your life that you're drawn to do that gives you the feeling of goodness, you have to prioritize it and do it often. You could even look at it as a kind of self-care. Doing what's meaningful to you regularly makes that thing a larger part of your life. By spending more time doing it, you're building it up, investing in it, and weaving it into your identity. Continuing this practice over some time builds meaning into your life because you've bonded with something inside of you that naturally makes you feel good.

After some time, you'll create a feedback loop of goodness. By figuring out what's meaningful to you and doing it consistently over time, you'll start to feel good about yourself for creating and maintaining meaning in your life. That's when you feel a sense of *purpose.* Now that you've created meaning and identified a feeling of your purpose in life (which is to do what feels meaningful), you start to feel a sense of *fulfillment.* You feel that way because you went through a self-discovery process, figured out what made you feel good, and intentionally followed it through. And if we look back to how we arrived at the word *fulfillment,* we'll see why this is a good place to land. We said we would want to feel *at ease, not hung up on small problems, satisfied, and good about what we've accomplished in life—with an optimistic outlook on the future.* Following the map we just went over will do exactly that.

The existential happiness we long for is the *afterglow* of feeling fulfilled. That means there's a bit of a recipe for creating a sustained feeling of happiness. We have to find something meaningful to us, make it a big part of our lives by devoting time to it, and then maintain the effort and love we pour into it. Doing this creates a perpetual cycle of action, meaning, and fulfillment. We'll then have a constant afterglow of happiness, bringing light to each moment in the present along with our view of the future.

> **In other words, if you want to be happy, prioritize doing things in life that make you feel alive. And make sure it isn't something *other people* say should bring you joy. Forget what other people think and do exactly what gives you that feeling like nothing else. Then do it again and again.**

Build it into your life. Make it important. By putting effort into what gives you life, you'll glow with the aura we have such a hard time describing because it's a feeling beyond words.

Finding Meaning through Growth

Now, I wouldn't walk you out on a longish philosophical ledge and just leave you there looking to the horizon with a pit in your stomach, wondering where you're going to find yourself some meaning. There's a reason I started this chapter by sharing how you can learn to use your open awareness as a tool for self-discovery.

You're already on a path. You're searching inside of yourself for ways to improve your life because you believe that a better life is possible no matter where you're at. You know that you aren't done growing—nor do you want to be—because you understand that you have the power to elevate your life. Being on this path is one of the largest potential builders of meaning you can ask for. As you look inward and continue to grow, you will create meaning, purpose, fulfillment, and happiness.

You decided to start your journey of growth and self-betterment. That means learning how to grow is important and makes you feel good. So the more that you continue to look inward and evolve, the more meaningful the act of doing that will become. As you see and feel the results of your efforts, you'll start to feel a sense of purpose. That purpose is to care for yourself and use your insight to improve your life experience. Doing this consistently will make your self-development crystal clear because you'll have a long period of time to look back on and contrast who you used to be with who you are in the present. Seeing this beautiful and healthy self-transformation will give you a feeling of fulfillment, igniting the afterglow of happiness.

Understanding this is powerful. When you see that the work you're doing on yourself to become happier is the exact thing that will lead to actual happiness, inner growth becomes effortless. It makes it so that you're simultaneously fueled and drawn by the same pursuit. In this way, you can live the rest of your life, making every one of your days better than the last while experiencing an unshakable sense of well-being.

CHAPTER 8

BE MINDFUL OF WHO YOU'RE WITH

There's a saying that you are a combination of your five closest friends. If you reflect on this one for a while, you'll find that it's likely spot-on. When considering what qualities you share with the people you choose to keep close to you, you'll notice that each offers something different.

You might talk about your inner life with one friend. Another could be someone you call when you want to grab a few cocktails and talk nonsense for a few hours. Yet another could be a friend with whom you share work and professional strategies. Someone else may be the person you reach out to when you want to go for a hike and talk about the big questions in life. However this looks for you, you'll notice that each of the closest people to you is a slice of who you are as a whole.

The "five people" thought experiment works because we seek friends who resonate with us. At the end of the day, we all want to be seen, find connections, and be able to share a sense with another person that we're experiencing a piece of what it means to be human—*together.* Bonding like this gives us a feeling of safety, energy, and relief. It makes us feel safe because we have someone we can trust to listen to us honestly without worrying about being judged. It excites us because we know we'll think of new perspectives and charge up with good energy when we're with them. And it makes us feel relieved because having someone in our lives that we can count on makes us feel less alone and well supported.

> **Connections are priceless. Yet it's a good practice to consider precisely how we're influenced by the people we spend time with. Most relationships we've had for a while plant deep roots in our lives. This makes us pay less attention to how we, and they, are showing up in the relationship and how it might have changed for the better or worse.**

Relationships can change so gradually—especially over the years—that it can be hard to recognize the changes as they happen. Looking at our relationships with a critical eye could seem cynical. It's not. It's being realistic and taking charge of who you want to be. And don't forget there are often positive outcomes of thinking about these things that make our relationships even deeper and more meaningful.

Who we spend our time with has a bigger impact on who we are than we often realize. People constantly absorb each other's thinking habits, perspectives, and behaviors. Think about the last time you watched a movie, series, or podcast and heard someone say a unique phrase or talk in a novel way. How many times have you gone on to parrot that phrase, perspective, or pronunciation style in your daily life as if it's your own? It's wild how much we're influenced by the energy we're around. Think about how an entertainer you watch on a glass screen for an hour can impact you. Then consider how much a friend you spend years with can shape your thoughts and feelings.

> **Being mindful of who we spend time with is essential to taking charge of who we are.**

Consider those five friends that you're a combination of. Would you be okay if you *were* one of those people? Do you strive to *be more like* some of those people? If you do, that's a beautiful friendship to hold on to. Feeling this way means that the person represents something good, inspirational, and wise and is helping you become more of who you want to be. On the other hand, if someone close to you constantly makes you feel bad about yourself or pulls you into destructive situations, it's worth considering why you still allow them to be close to you and if those patterns are what you want for your future self.

Good Relationships Need Energy

When we're around people who inspire, support, and trust us, it creates a momentum you can't find anywhere else. Healthy relationships with friends, partners, and colleagues give us the energy, belief, and guidance that help us get to where we want to be. If you were to live in France for a year, you'd pick up much of the language, customs, and mindset of the people from the country. It doesn't even take effort. It just happens naturally through social osmosis. Now, consider if everyone you keep close to you is positive, honest, motivated, and self-aware. If that's who you spend most of your time with, then just like living in France, you're going to pick up the mental habits of all those people. By simply being around them, your mindset will shift, and you'll start to feel more positive, motivated, and conscious. That's why you need to choose who you spend time with wisely.

Mindfully Pick Your Pack

We have the power to choose who we're close to. Of course, in professional settings, we might have to engage with people who don't have the energy we'd hope to be around. That's fine and circumstantial. Those relationships can remind you of who you *don't want* to be. However, we can decide who we want to be around in our personal lives. We can choose which friends, partners, or family members to spend time with.

> **Like an art museum curates a gallery, we can curate the people in our lives. We can consciously choose who we want to be close to so we can be intentional about who influences us.**

Don't worry if this sounds heavy. It doesn't have to be. You're just picking your pack instead of allowing randomness and chaos to rule your relationships.

When you consider the people you know, think about how they make you feel.

- Do you feel comfortable when you're with them?
- Do they make you feel good about yourself?
- Are they honest with you in a caring way?
- Do they introduce you to new things that inspire you?
- Do they consistently set goals and reach them?
- Do they reach out to you as much as you do to them?
- Are they on the same path of growth that you're on?
- Can you count on them when you need them?

If a person you know has wholesome qualities like these, you would be wise to spend as much time as you can with them to invite good energy into your life.

On the other hand, if some relationships don't make you feel good, it's important to listen to what you're feeling. Some signs of negative relationships to watch for:

- You feel anxious around them and unwelcome.
- You never feel like they give you their full attention.
- You feel like an accessory to their lives.
- You know that they haven't been honest with you.
- They play you and other people against each other.
- They are controlling and don't care about your opinion.
- You observe them treating other people poorly.
- You are always the one who reaches out to connect.

If you have relationships with this kind of energy, then it's important to be honest about them. These relationships may not have been that way when you got into them, or maybe you've grown while the other person hasn't. Whatever the case, you have to confront the fact that by remaining close in that relationship, you are *choosing* to bring that energy into your life. And by doing that, it means that you're subtly absorbing the qualities you dislike, which will shape who you are in the future.

Mindfully picking your pack is a powerful practice. Looking at your relationships in an insightful way helps you understand what type of environment you're placing yourself in. Then, with that awareness, you can consciously decide what energy, habits, and perspective you want to surround yourself with.

Choosing who you're around is a continuous process. People change. You change. So being mindful of where things are at is wise. Doing this allows you to influence yourself by choosing who is around to influence you.

Good Relationships Give Good Energy

Good relationships are invaluable. They keep us going, inspire us, and make us feel connected. Some of the best ones are constant sources of energy. I've always thought this is a strange phenomenon and like to reflect on it often. How can we go out with a friend, spend all night talking, laughing, and burning energy, and somehow wake up feeling *more* energized than if we'd stayed home to rest? I think it's because many kinds of energy are available to us, yet we don't always consider them all. We usually think about energy in terms of getting sleep, proper nutrition, and time to recharge at home. While those certainly contribute to our energy levels, they have more to do with the mechanical nature of our beings.

Another type of energy, something closer to *universal vitality*, drives us in a way that can be much more potent than getting a few extra hours of sleep. This energy is connected to our mindset. When we let go while feeling optimistic, prepared, and hungry for the future, a type of *cosmic wind* blows at our backs. Being powered by this force is how we can get into higher gears of living and drop into a perpetual flow state of presence, brilliance, and clarity. Lieh Tzu, a lesser-known Taoist philosopher, suggested we should learn to "ride the wind and float with the clouds." I believe the feeling I described is what he was pointing to.

I've found that when you spend time with the right people, the synergy created between you and them can bring this energy to life. This can happen even with someone you don't know well. Over the years, I've talked with hundreds of people on my podcast. Certainly not every time, but sometimes, I would get enough energy from that conversation to last several days, if not longer. Connections like these are like two ends of a battery meeting at the perfect moment. Separately, they have some power, but when you put them together, they create something bigger than the sum of the parts—and a whole new wave of energy becomes available.

If someone in your life makes you feel more energized after you spend time with them, you should not take that for granted. Actually, you should make it a priority to spend time with that person regularly.

> **It's an incredible gift when you find the right friend or partner who gives you life. And if they feel the same energy too—it's a priceless connection.**

Zooming out and thinking about the energy flow in your relationships is fascinating. I've noticed three distinct styles.

- **Upward Flow:** These connections you have are guaranteed to feed you. When you spend time with this person, you always walk away having learned something, feeling supported, or being energized. However, the other person doesn't feel the same. These relationships are good for you but can be draining for the person giving their energy to you.

- **Downward Flow:** In these relationships, you always feel drained and picked over afterward. When you're with this type of person, you feel like you're giving without getting anything in return. It doesn't mean that you dislike people who drain you. It's simply apparent that you consistently feel low on energy after you're with them.

- **Synergetic Flow:** These relationships are golden. When you spend time together, *both* of you feel more energized. You can connect uniquely, bringing something special out in both of you. It creates an endless flow of ideas, positive vibes, and energy. These are people who can become lifelong friends or partners.

Being aware of the energy flow in relationships is helpful. It clarifies how much time is appropriate to share with them, not only for your benefit but for theirs as well.

Throughout my life, I've intentionally sought out friends with whom I have a synergetic connection. Obviously, I'm not interested in being drained by anyone, so I severely limit the time I spend around people who leave me feeling like an empty buffet. If someone only hits you up when they need something, they aren't your friend. You are their food. And if I don't feel like I'm providing much in return to someone in a relationship, I limit the time I spend with them. The last thing I want to be is an accidental energy vampire, so I choose times to engage with those people wisely.

Now, I feel super grateful to have about half a dozen friends in my life that are highly synergetic relationships. Whenever I talk to or hang out with them, I feel a wave of energy that stays with me for days. It keeps me flowing along, riding the wind, feeling inspired to keep ascending with a smile. And I know it leaves them feeling that way too. As I mentioned, these special relationships didn't happen by accident. I cultivated them over a long time—years, really. The key is being mindful of what you feel when you're with someone, then intentionally leaning in to that relationship when you can tell something special is happening there. As you do this over a long period, you'll start to collect relationships like these and find yourself with an incredible crew of special humans.

Building up several relationships like these is a real form of magic. By having many people in your life who *give you more life,* you can naturally cycle through your engagements with them. By doing so, you will surely give yourself a steady flow of the *universal vitality* I mentioned earlier. Intelligently constructing powerful friendships and partnerships like these not only keeps you happy, inspired, and energized—it lifts up the quality of your whole life.

Leave Behind Bad Connections

Staying in bad relationships is one of the most common—yet most overlooked—things that cause suffering in people's lives. By relationships, I mean romantic partnerships, friendships, and even connections with family members. We are taught that if we don't hold on to our relationships, we are somehow a "bad person." Also, no one wants to be alone, so we can grow an innate fear of letting relationships go, even if they're bad, because we'd rather be with someone who doesn't treat us well than no one at all.

We should face the facts. If we aren't being fed, we're probably being eaten. Taking a realistic look at how healthy or unhealthy our connections are will change our lives. Like our thinking habits, we get so used to how things feel with certain people that we accept them as "how things are" and forget that other ways of living are possible. But this is no good. The people in our lives have an incredible influence over how we feel, think, and act.

That raises the question: Why would we allow someone else to be a harmful presence in our lives?

1. **Numbness.** When we meet someone, they and we are both at a certain place in our lives. As time passes, some people grow, and others don't. People who don't grow will do nothing but keep you down and create a negative influence in your life. However, we can have a hard time seeing reality for what it is because we remain attached to the memory of who someone *was* or what they represented to us at one time, as opposed to who they are today.

   Staying attached to this memory preys on our empathy. Because we still think of this person as who they *were,* we consider that historical version of them as the one we would be leaving behind if we created distance in the relationship. This is why we ignore or make excuses for a person's negative behavior. Our reality isn't synced with the present moment, so we can't see clearly.

   In such situations, it's useful to ask yourself: If you met this person as who they are *today,* would you want to build a relationship with them?

2. **Fear.** When we are aware that someone is a bad connection in our life but continue to spend time with them anyway, we do so out of fear. Everyone wants to belong. It's etched in our DNA to find a

group of people and stick with the pack. However, sometimes we can get into bad situations where we change who we are to fit in out of desperation. Or we might allow a knowingly negative force to persist because we don't want to lose someone and feel alone.

Whatever the case, staying in relationships out of fear or codependency destroys your self-worth, mental clarity, and physical health. You're worth more than that. And you can find new people you align with who positively influence your life. It feels scary to leave behind a connection when you may not have many. But here's a truth I can share from experience with you.

The courage it takes to leave behind what's not for you anymore is the same courage that will help you find your way to what is.

3. **Family.** Dealing with toxic family members is one of the most challenging things we can face. Distancing ourselves from people we are supposed to love—and who are supposed to love us—feels counterintuitive. It's like doing a simple math problem where the numbers won't add up. That's because we all want to believe that people connected to us by blood will always come around, become self-aware, and change for the better. Sadly, that's not true. There's also an unspoken rule in society that pressures us to stick with our birth families even if they are a destructive presence in our lives.

   The reality is that a family member is still a person. There's nothing special about them that will magically keep them from treating you poorly. And just because they came from the same gene pool and shared a few formative experiences with you doesn't give them a pass to lay a lifetime of unchecked toxicity on you. They are an adult person and need to respect you like everyone else—or they don't deserve access to you.

If you're aware of people in your life who are a negative presence, it's wise to consider taking steps to confront that truth head-on. Otherwise, nothing will change. You both will continue going around and around in the same patterns. You'll keep taking their negativity, and it will continue to limit your happiness, dampen your potential, and drain your mental energy.

Unless the situation is extreme, you shouldn't simply cut off contact with people with a negative place in your life. Circumstances always vary, but leading with thoughtfulness, compassion, and lack of assumption is usually the best way to start.

Don't just dump people and move on. Talk to them first. Tell them how you feel, what kind of presence they are in your life, and what you need from them. Ask them if they're willing to change. Sometimes, this person could be oblivious to how they are treating you, and your conversation could be an insightful, healing, and bonding moment for both of you. Other times, they may not be willing to hear you and take responsibility for their actions. They could react with anger, manipulation, victimhood, or gaslighting. If that's the case, then you know that you've given them a chance, and it's time to set *firm* boundaries and put space in the relationship to protect yourself.

There can be a feeling of mourning that goes along with leaving behind bad connections or relationships that simply don't align anymore. Sometimes we might even wonder if we did something wrong that caused a fracture in the connection. It's natural to feel that way, but it's important to remember that most relationships are seasonal. Few people will be in our lives forever. We meet people at certain moments in our lives, are aligned, and spend time together. As time passes, our interests change, we grow in different directions, and the resonance that we once found in each other goes quiet.

Many relationships are like two boats traveling across the ocean, both set with different starting and ending coordinates. We started in different places, and for a while, we crossed paths. But in the end, we were headed to different destinations. There's nothing wrong with that. It's natural. And while it's easy to reminisce and feel down about relationships we've had to leave behind, there's another way to look at it. We can be grateful that we met those people when we did. That we were able to share beautiful moments, learn from each other, and help each other along that leg of our journeys. We wouldn't be who we are today without meeting them then. And although those memories are precious, we are capable and will go on to create more meaningful moments with new people in the future.

CHAPTER 9

CHANGE YOUR SPEECH, CHANGE YOUR REALITY

Research shows that the average person speaks 7,000 words a day. That means we spend at least one hour of our day talking. Depending on your lifestyle and profession, these numbers could double or even quadruple. So if you have to talk in meetings at work or have a busy social life, you can easily speak 15,000 words a day without breaking a sweat. That means you say the entire text of almost two 240-page books every week. It's wild when you really think about it. Listening to an audiobook feels like a lot. But that's how much time we spend talking every week.

We're chatty creatures. That's because speech is our superpower. The human ability to communicate complexly is how we got so smart. So smart, in fact, that those smarts snagged us a comfortable seat at the top of the food chain. Not only do we like to talk, we *have to* talk. And with good reason. Talking is how we understand ourselves. By saying our thoughts *out into the world,* we can see the contents of our minds from a new point of view. Doing this gives us perspective. It's like audio journaling. It's also why we sometimes surprise ourselves when an idea we didn't know we had comes out of our mouths.

When we talk, we're also imprinting our perspective on the world. Talking is like a form of hypnosis. It is how we negotiate, craft, and integrate reality. We talk casually about facts, possibilities, meaning, and what's "real" all day. Sharing our take with others in this way influences how they think, shifting how they see the world, themselves, and us.

Even with all this talking, we rarely stop and think about how impactful our words are. They genuinely have the power to shift reality, create meaning, and spark emotions. Yet we are so used to talking that we often overlook its magic.

How Our Words Shape Reality

Think about words as symbols. They are sounds that represent meaning. When we use words, we are communicating something about reality to others. How we put those words together creates a story about what's true. That story, like any good story, is attractive and gripping. So when we talk, we persuade others to see the world the way we see it.

However, it isn't that simple. The meaning that words represent is different for all of us. That means that even though we might be saying what we mean, other people don't hear it that way. They hear it in a way that means something to them—not us. This misalignment of perception is how miscommunications happen. One person thinks the other hears what they are saying in the way they mean it. The other person thinks they hear what the person who is talking means. Both are wrong.

What We Say Should Be What We Mean

It's important to be mindful of what you say. You can't know how someone is going to take your words. A passing comment could land wrong and make someone feel unsure of themselves. A careless joke could come off as sincere and actually hurt. An exaggerated story could make someone lose trust in your view of reality.

> **Appreciating that what we say has a more powerful effect on other people than we realize will help us choose our words wisely and instill goodwill, harmony, and kindness in everyone we speak with.**

Being present while talking will help us think more clearly, show up how we intend, and more accurately convey what we mean.

How We Say Things Should Be Genuine

Nuance plays a big role in our communication. Sometimes we say words that mean one thing but say them with a tone that means something totally different. Whatever am I talking about? <wink> Let's be real. When we're angry, annoyed, or anxious, it's tempting to add a twang to our words that gives them a pungent energy. Doing this is like using a cheat code. It's a safe way to express straightforward negativity because it has a built-in escape hatch.

For example, we might say something factual but with a sarcastic tone. The intention is to be able to express our authentic emotions behind the safety of real words. If someone questions our tone, we can then be manipulative and claim we didn't mean to sound sarcastic. Not a cool thing to do.

Tone is so delicate in our speech that people use and abuse its power all the time. Some people even make a sport out of it. However, we shouldn't do this. It's just as bad for the person speaking as it is for the person listening. It harms other people because it gaslights them by trying to manipulate their impression of reality. And it's harmful to us because it bottles our emotions, prohibits us from expressing ourselves, and brews internal negativity that gets carried with us long after we make the comments.

The good news is that the tone of our speech cuts both ways. We can use its power to bring loads of positivity into our lives and those around us. Being mindful of speaking in an authentic way keeps our integrity strong. Talking without an air of negativity builds trust with people. Showing up this way creates stability in relationships that makes people feel safe in your presence. When someone feels safe, it helps them let go, open up, and share the essence of who they are.

> **Deep trust builds deep relationships. By speaking authentically, you not only build confidence with other people, but you build confidence within yourself.**

Where We Speak from Matters

For years, I've been fascinated with where people speak from. It's one of the things that's always on my radar. Listening to where people are speaking from opens up this whole new dimension of communication. I'd never really thought to share that I do this until it came up in a recent conversation with a friend. When I shared my thoughts on it, he was super intrigued, and it made me realize it'd be something worthwhile to pass along to others, as it can be quite an illuminating practice.

Here goes, and keep in mind I was a professional music producer for over a decade, so I think of sound in terms of three-dimensional vibration instead of just noise. Over the years, I noticed that some people speak from their *sinuses*, others speak from their *throats*, and others speak from the center of their *chests*.

From what I can sense, the origin of a person's voice generates a unique kind of energy. We can sense this when we're talking to them. If we pay attention, we can see a correlation between where a person is speaking from and the current state of their *inner landscape*—that is, the complex world of feelings, thoughts, and perspectives swirling around in them at that moment.

A person speaking from their face feels tight, unsure, and anxious. The mind-body connection creates this. When a person becomes tense, only the tiniest opening is available to eke out words at the top of their body. Someone speaking from their throat feels normal and balanced, often with a passive level of engagement to the present. People most commonly speak from this place. A person speaking from their chest is open, rich, and confident. You can feel the presence of someone talking like this on a deep level. Sensations of truth, wisdom, awareness, and strength often radiate from them.

How This Is Helpful

The more you start watching for this, the more you'll notice it. After some practice, it can become an intuitive part of feeling into other people. It's like a wordless window into the deeper truth of another person's words.

To break this down further, I will put it another way. Think about this phenomenon in terms of *vibration*. What do you hear when you listen to music that would play well as the soundtrack to a horror movie? Tension. Dissonance. Contraction. These sounds intentionally vibrate in broken, harsh, and conflicting ways. They are composed that way to create emotional distress. The end goal is that the music will add to the on-screen tension and increase the film's impact on you.

Now, think about the music you hear that accompanies a guided meditation. What do you hear? Release. Expansion. Calm. Long and fluid sounds that blend into each other with no clear beginning or end. This music is also composed with a purpose in mind. Its purpose is to vibrate at a slow, smooth, and consistent pace.

Ambient music is relaxing because it allows you to *trust* it. The longer you listen, the more it builds confidence that there will be no surprises, sudden jolts, or critical changes. This trust lets you surrender to the sound and completely let go.

Now, let's return to the awareness of vibration in voice. After considering how different music vibrates with varying emotional impacts, consider how it relates to speech. You'll notice that someone speaking from high in their head has dissonance similar to music designed to create tension. Because the person's body is tight, their breath is short, and their mind is racing, the vibration of their voice will convey tension the same way that music does.

This awareness can be helpful because it's a beautiful opportunity to feel empathy, compassion, and understanding on a new level. When you feel the tension in someone's voice, it's an invisible sign that they are suffering. Being aware of this gives you a chance to show up for them. You can ask them how they are doing, try to talk out what's on their mind, or be a calm companion in the present moment.

> **Learning to feel the vibration in other people's voices is like a superpower.**

You don't have to bring it up. You don't have to reveal that you can feel the energy beneath their words. All you have to do is use that new dimension of awareness to understand people more deeply and help lift up their lives when the time feels right.

Tuning In to Deep Speech

Let's turn this idea of voice as vibration around on ourselves. If you could choose, what kind of "music" would you want to play from you when you talk? Chances are you'd pick the description of the ambient music from above. I'm assuming you'd pick that choice because speaking from a deep, grounded, and wise place radiates a calm, safe, and aware sensation you can *feel*. Being around people like this is a beautiful, healing, and inviting experience.

How do they give off that feeling?

They are feeling the feeling they are giving off on the inside.

Good news. You can cultivate this feeling for yourself. Speaking from an intentional place shifts the texture of your mind similarly to when you are chanting a meditation mantra. Here are some steps to help you tune in to the deepest connection to your voice.

First, I'd say that you should experiment with this while you are alone. Doing this will allow you to open up and play without feeling restrained, shy, or worried that anyone is going to think you're too weird.

Now, we're going to start talking.

What you are saying isn't important right now.

Where you are saying it from is.

Start repeating your full name out loud again and again. Keep saying it as if it's on a loop.

Speak out loud and focus on your face as if it's where your voice starts. Feel how ungrounded, restricted, and unsure it feels. Spend 5 or 10 seconds doing this while studying the sensations.

Next, continue repeating your name out loud, but allow the place where your voice begins to drop lower.

Move the starting point into your throat.

You'll feel a bit more control, some expansion, and focus.

Now, relax the muscles in your neck, shoulders, and chest. Then, move the starting point of your voice down into the center of your chest.

While you talk, let go, open up, and feel your voice connecting to something more profound.

Practice speaking from this deep place for 10 to 20 seconds.

Your body might start to become tense and try to tighten up again. That's fine. It's just its current habit. If this happens, relax your muscles again, take calming breaths, and speak from your chest.

Feel into the depth of your voice. Notice how speaking from your chest helps you relax in your skin more and more. Watch how your mind gets clearer, your focus sharpens, and your confidence firms.

Once you feel comfortable and have built a relationship with your voice, practice speaking from this place while talking with others. You'll notice you feel strong, grounded, and patient in conversation. You won't chatter for no reason. You will speak with force, precision, and purpose. The more consistent you are with remembering to speak from your chest, the more natural it will become. In time, it will be instinctual.

Developing this self-connection is a gift.

> **Speaking from deep within is a form of *intentional* self-change, just like the mantra chant during meditation. However, in this case, the chant is the tone of your own voice, grounding and clearing your mind every time you speak.**

Doing this will not only contribute to your ability to feel greater confidence, clarity, and presence, it will radiate outward. Everyone you speak with, whether conscious of it or not, will feel the calm, clear, and healing nature of your voice's vibration.

Your words shape reality. By speaking from an intentionally self-connected place, you can bend the shape of reality to favor the positive, expansive, present, and kind.

Mindful Communication

Given that our words are so powerful, learning to be mindful when we speak creates a huge opportunity for growth. Think about when someone you care about says something mean to you. Consider how much it hurts, how long it sticks with you, and how it pulls you down. It's a terrible feeling that can push you off your path and break relationships.

Ah, but there's a flip side. If that kind of impact is real with hurtful words, then *the same is true for their opposite.* By being mindful when we speak, we can choose words that create big waves of positivity inside others and ourselves. With little effort, we can make people feel good, lift them up, and fill them with a feeling of warmth.

Start by trying to employ these techniques when you remember. As you continue to apply yourself, these practices will become automatic. One day, it will hit you that you're speaking mindfully without even trying, and you'll realize that you've permanently leveled up your awareness.

How to Mindfully Communicate

1. Don't repeatedly bring the focus of the conversation back on you.

Since we express ourselves when we talk, focusing only on our takes, feelings, and interests is natural. Doing this can make the other person feel unimportant, disconnected, and small.

Making sure a conversation is balanced deepens connections. Allow space while you're talking. Listen to what they say instead of waiting for your turn to speak. Inviting the other person to share more helps them feel safe and allows them to go deeper into themselves. Doing these things creates a channel between two people that enables them to hear each other, connect on a deep level, and for a moment become one.

2. Ask questions instead of correcting people.

Most of us have a firm attachment to how we think things are. Because of this, we are quick to react and correct other people's opinions during a conversation.

> **Building the habit of asking questions instead of correcting people is a strong form of mindful communication. It keeps you from making assumptions and gives the person you're talking to a chance to share more of their insights, which often leads to valuable new ways of thinking.**

3. Quietly listen.

During the heat of a conversation, we often get excited and share our opinions at length. While this can be appropriate sometimes, it's wise to be mindful of when or why we contribute our point of view.

> **Sometimes quietly listening can be more powerful than speaking. We don't always need to be the ones giving opinions. Being patient and giving our attention to the person we are talking with will often make them feel more validated than anything we could say.**

It will make them feel heard and give them the space to open up.

4. Communicate boundaries.

Speaking isn't limited to friendly chats. Words are tools you can and should use to let others know your feelings and where you stand. Be clear about what you're comfortable with. People aren't mind readers. You have to tell them what your boundaries are before they can know.

Be clear about how much time you can give. Carving out time in your day to focus on what's important to you is the only way to progress. Not everyone is on the same path or has the same obligations as you do. So they might be more flexible with their time and not realize they aren't respecting yours. You should also be clear about what's meaningful to you. Each of us has different things in life that give us our purpose. Sometimes you need to express this to others, so they better understand why you do what you do.

> **Communicating your boundaries is how you define your life. It lets other people know who you are and makes it clear if they try to treat you as someone you are not.**

5. Let go of the urge to say harmful things.

We all have an instinct now and again to talk trash, gossip, or put things down. While this is a natural part of being human, being mindful of speaking this way is important.

> **Here's a simple way to improve your life: when you feel you're about to say something negative for no reason, pause and let it go.**

Speaking negatively doesn't add anything good to how you or the people around you feel. It only encourages the energy of the conversation to become more harmful.

Also, the patterns that you speak in influence the habits that you think in. That's because the neuroplasticity of our brains shifts to make what we do easier. So if you often say negative things, you will think negatively. Not just about others but about yourself and your potential future. Resisting the urge to speak in a critical, harmful, and judgmental way literally rewires your brain's synapses. That means the longer you practice this, the fewer negative thoughts will rise in your mind throughout the day.

6. Speak from a sincere and present place.

It's obvious when someone isn't tuned in or placates you during a conversation. This energy keeps people from connecting and invites the potential for subtle sarcasm and negativity.

Be sincere when you speak. It conveys an authentic energy that grounds the conversation. What's lovely about this is that creating a firm and open feeling in a conversation gives the person you're talking to a feeling of trust. This feeling allows them to access deeper parts of themselves, share more, and embrace a rich sense of realness.

7. Choose your words as you speak.

Because we speak so much, it's easy to drift and start speaking on autopilot. Paying attention to what you're saying as you're saying it is a strong form of mindful awareness. Doing this doesn't take any extra energy. All it takes is attention. And practicing this comes with a big reward. Being mindful of your words as you speak helps you clarify your thoughts. This clarity will help you express yourself more precisely, reducing the chance of miscommunication and increasing your ability to convey what's meaningful to you.

Choosing what you say with intention also helps you speak honestly. Sometimes we can be hyperbolic, bend the truth, or hide ulterior motivations in our words. Being aware of what you're saying prevents this, which boosts your integrity and makes others see you as trustworthy. Paying attention to your words also gives you the space to prioritize kindness. It's incredible how even the most minor kind comments can greatly impact other people. Often much more than we could ever know.

8. Being peaceful doesn't mean you're always passive.

It's important to assert yourself sometimes. Of course, it's healthy to be rational and nonreactionary. However, life sometimes gets thick, and we aren't heard or face unfair resistance. In these moments, we need to put power in our words and make a claim to our lives.

When you are assertive, speak kindly but honestly. There's no need to be angry or negative when being forceful. You just need to be clear and matter-of-fact without attachment to aggressive emotions. Speaking like this when needed fosters a sense of self-belief, makes you feel validated, and helps you give yourself the respect you deserve.

PART III

NEW VIEW, NEW YOU

CHAPTER 10

DON'T SETTLE

The longer we live, the deeper we settle into grooves. Some of these grooves are good. We can figure out what we like, and dislike, what brings us joy, and what makes our skin crawl. What's interesting is that a lot of these grooves form without us having much say in the matter. It's like while we were busy trying to live, our life formed into something on its own, and we were just caught up in the middle of the commotion.

We get this feeling that our lives turned out differently than we'd planned because we're always adapting. While we're living, micro-changes happen bit by bit. We meet new people, take on new behavior habits, start hanging around different places, or get busy with new activities to pass the days. Over time, these things gradually shift the shape of our lives, who we are, and how we think of ourselves.

While this is natural, the deep sense that it happens *outside of our control* gives us the feeling that we don't have any say in what our lives should be. Things take on the appearance of being locked in, final, and unchangeable. In time, we trick ourselves into accepting our reality as "the way things are" and stop trying to intervene and make our lives better. The longer this goes on, the more normalized our existence feels. Even the things that make us unhappy that we wish we could change start to look like "features" of life that are unavoidable. The aspirations we have yet to achieve also take on the feeling of being out of touch. Because our life seems to take shape on its own, we resign ourselves to the notion that we can't achieve greatness—whatever that means to us.

You Have the Power

The good news is that even though you may *think* you can't take charge of your life and bend reality in your favor, it isn't true. Believing this is a simple thought habit that has formed over a long period of time. So long, in fact, that it's possible you've forgotten other ways of thinking are possible.

> **The truth is that nothing is unchangeable. You have the power to change how you see and engage with your life at any time.**

You can choose to work on your mental health, improve your physical health, or go all in on achieving your dream goals. *Your attachment to the idea that this isn't true* is the only thing holding you back. Now, I know that might sound like some self-help gobbledygook. Fortunately for both of us, it isn't.

Think about every great thing that's happened in your life. Those things only happened because your *mindset* was tuned to a state of belief and forward movement. You released your attachment to the idea that what you did wasn't possible and made it so with your unwillingness to be limited by negative thinking habits. Improving other parts of your life is only a matter of applying that mindset shift and force of belief to a different problem. The only requirement is that you *actually* have to leave behind your old way of thinking, *believe,* and take action.

All the ways of thinking that make you feel heavy like you're wearing a lead robe—you know, like self-critical thoughts, negative mental stories, and bad assumptions about reality—pull you down. They suck your energy, dry up your inspiration, and make you believe that *less is possible.*

Let's look at some common *external* ways of thinking that could be holding you back and some alternate perspectives.

Professional:

Problem: What you're doing, the mission of your work, the people you work with, the amount of energy you put into your work, or your lack of work-life balance all feel like they are unchangeable, and there's no other road to take.

Solution: One approach could be to seek a new appreciation for the work you're already doing. Try going back in time. Remember why you started doing the work in the first place. See if that doesn't realign your perception or help you see your work in a refreshed light. Another option is to start looking for a new job in your free time in the evening. The good thing is that you can often get a higher salary when transferring to a new company while already employed. Create work-life balance by setting firm boundaries for yourself. Don't bring work home with you or reply to e-mails while not at work unless it's a crucial exception.

Relationships:

Problem: You don't feel connected to your friends, your partner doesn't feel like an ally, your professional relationships are transactional, and your family is an unhealthy force that doesn't respect your boundaries.

Solution: Be proactive and reach out to your friends more often. Friendships are two-sided relationships; the more time you spend together, the more you bond. Talk with your partner about wanting to feel like they are on your side. They may not realize you feel this way or that it's important to you. Limit your contact with toxic people and create firm boundaries to give your life the respect it deserves.

Lack of exercise and poor diet:

Problem: You don't feel strong and resilient, you don't feel good about your appearance, your energy suffers, and you feel like you can't get into a habit of eating well.

Solution: Do research, find an exercise plan that works for you, and stick to it for at least three months so you can see clear improvement. If you don't feel keen on exercising, your solution could be as simple as making better choices when eating and keeping track of your daily calories. Getting in better shape is all about patience and self-accountability. Make progress, not excuses.

Wrong environment:

Problem: You feel disconnected and bored with where you live, the weather doesn't suit your natural inclination, and the culture around you doesn't feel exciting or inviting.

Solution: Try exploring new places in the city where you live. Look around online and find bars, restaurants, etc., that you haven't been to before and experiment *without expectations*. You'll find a whole world out there and plenty of stuff for everyone. Make it a point to travel a few times a year to the climates you enjoy and center your trip around hiking and outdoor activities.

Feeling stuck:

Problem: You think you have no plan for the future, there are no goals you want to accomplish, and you feel like you're drifting and can't find your way.

Solution: There's a saying that goes, "If you have writer's block, you just haven't done enough research." The same applies here. Expand your horizons, get curious, and start openly trying things you'd never considered trying before. You'll be amazed at how the most unexpected experiences can resonate. For example, I would have never thought I loved making pasta from scratch. But for some reason, I tried it one day. Now whipping up some tremendous tagliatelle by hand is like a form of meditation for me.

Your self-limiting mindsets could also be *internal* things, like these.

No direction on your inner path:

Problem: You feel that you don't know where to go next and you have reached the depth of your spiritual self-understanding.

Solution: Look deeper into the teachings you've studied so far. Read the books that the books you've read are based on. Learn about new wisdom traditions, listen to new lectures, and switch up the teachers that you follow.

No time or discipline to meditate:

Problem: You feel like you can't meditate, so you don't try, which makes your mental clarity and inner peace suffer.

Solution: Lower the stakes on what you think *successful* meditation has to look like. Take a meditation course or find a local meditation center to attend. Everyone can meditate. You just have yet to receive proper guidance that works for you.

Limiting beliefs about your potential:

Problem: You believe you can't bring your dreams to life, and it isn't in the cards for you to do so.

Solution: Consider that you may no longer have passion for what you once thought was your main aspiration. Explore your interests, find something that makes you feel alive, then pour your energy into it.

Negative view of relationships:

Problem: You see them as difficult work with no reward and believe you're better off isolating yourself from friends or potential partners.

Solution: Humans are pack animals. Consider speaking with a therapist to understand why you desire isolation, then work to rebuild healthy relationships.

If one of these ideas rings true to your life, consider this: It seems true because it's how things have been for a long time, or as long as you can remember. You've normalized this part of your life as something given, unchangeable, and final. Remember, nothing is final. It only appears that way because you've *stopped questioning your reality.*

You can let go of what's holding you down.

You can move anything blocking your path.

You can heal anything that's hurting you.

You can change anything in your life.

All you have to do is *choose* to let go of the idea that your life is already determined. Then *choose* to believe you can grow in all the ways you can imagine. Then take action and start turning your vision into a reality.

Don't Mistake Passiveness for Peace

Now that we're in the neighborhood of talking about taking action, being forceful, and grabbing ahold of your own life, I want us to talk about a common misconception.

When we set out on a path of self-growth, that journey is often accompanied by a desire to bring more peace into our lives. We aim to move toward harmony in everything we do. While on this path—especially at the beginning—people actively *try* to be more peaceful. Now, there's absolutely nothing wrong with this, and I wish more people would do it. Being gentle with yourself and others is a great boon to the world. However, boons can go bad when they are misunderstood.

I've taught thousands of people meditation over the years and get messages and questions from them often. Something I started noticing is that people have a real knack for mistaking being *actively peaceful* with being passive. What that means is they avoid dealing with anger and stress by being passive, practicing avoidance, and mistaking that for inner balance.

Mistaking Detachment for Nonattachment

Taking on life with a high-minded perspective is a great way to deal with the *unchangeable* ups and downs we inevitably experience. Using distancing techniques—like zooming out our perspective to keep what really matters in mind—is a stellar way not to get emotionally banged up from clinging to things we can't control.

We call this *nonattachment.* Essentially, it means we don't get attached to how we see reality. We understand that everything changes, so we accept and flow with life's changes instead of resisting them. However, this idea is nuanced and often underexplained. Misunderstanding it can trick us into becoming passive in our lives, settling for "how things are," and mistaking it all for a peaceful approach to living.

For example, let's say that you want to start a podcast. You grab the gear, come up with a catchy theme, and start dropping episodes twice a week. After two months, you see the download numbers aren't breaking any records, and it bums you out. The discouragement unsettles your sense of inner peace. It makes you question your ability to do something you wanted, which makes you feel vulnerable and challenges how you see yourself. This isn't a pleasant feeling, but it's quite helpful—we'll get into that later in the book. Instead of moving through the tension you feel and understanding how you need to course correct, you bypass your thoughts and emotions, become passive, and mistake it for peacefulness. *Passive thoughts* we might use in a situation sound like this:

"Well, I guess I wasn't *meant* to be a podcaster."

"It's too hard to make a name for myself in a saturated market."

"I don't have time to record podcasts. It's too much work."

"You have to get lucky to build an audience."

In this situation, you are attempting to be peaceful or *unbothered* by something *not outside of your control.* Doing this undermines your ability to achieve your goals. It is how one gets into the habit of letting their life live them instead of them living their life. It's settling for "what is" instead of creating the outcome you desire.

Doing this is a form of *detachment.* It's giving ourselves a pass *not to play an active role in our own lives to preserve a false feeling of comfort.* After doing this, we tell ourselves a story about what happened to rewrite reality, rationalize our behavior, and move on. Of course, we mistake passiveness for peace in our emotional lives too. Whenever we're in conflict with someone else, and we feel tension, frustration, or sadness, it's easy to not stand up for our emotions in the name of being peaceful. Doing this simply represses the feeling instead of addressing it, causing you to bottle it up until it eventually explodes.

Whether it's dealing with goals or emotions, it's important for you to feel into the moment. Are you being passive because you don't want to temporarily feel healthy growing pains? Or are you legitimately nonattached to the situation and able to release any tension that arises with a clear conscience?

> **Give yourself the respect of taking action when it feels right. Not only will it make you happier and feel more confident, but it will also break the spell that things in life "are how they are" and give you the courage to take charge of your reality.**

CHAPTER 11

USE YOUR PAST TO POWER YOUR PRESENT

Hopefully, at this point, you've picked up some tools that have helped you take control of your thinking. Maybe you've already stopped some negative thinking habits dead in their tracks and began expanding your view of yourself and the world. After the last chapter, I hope you felt inspired to use your new outlook to start living as if more truly is possible for you.

If you're feeling that way, it's great news. It means you're gaining momentum and feeling motivated to take your life to the next level. Now, what's interesting is that at this stage, many people have the instinct to sort of "cut ties" with their old identity. By that, I mean that since they've become aware of how they want to move forward, they start trying to distance themselves from the idea of who they were. It's like they are trying to "cleanse" their sense of self. While this isn't necessarily bad, it leaves some valuable growth potential on the table.

> **Remembering where we are growing *from* helps us grow into who we want to become.**

One reason this is helpful is that internal change is so gradual. It all takes place in our minds, which means it can be tricky to tell if we're making any progress. Keeping an image in your memory of how you used to react, think, or feel in a certain situation is quite useful. You can use this memory to contrast how you think, feel, and act in the present. That way, you'll be able to tell if you're growing in the way you want or need to focus more effort in any other areas.

For example, say that in the past you always felt uncomfortable when talking with your partner about what you need to work on in your relationship. In most cases, it's not that you didn't want to improve the relationship. It's that talking about those things makes you feel vulnerable and anxious, which causes you to close off and communicate poorly. However, after noticing this behavior, you start to work on those thinking habits, ease yourself into vulnerable conversations, and build up self-trust. One day, you find yourself in the middle of a conversation with your partner about your relationship and notice that you feel positive and at ease with no sense of anxiety or tension. Then, comparing how you're comfortably communicating today with how you anxiously did in the past makes it clear how much you've grown.

Another reason keeping these mental snapshots is helpful is because it will keep you inspired. Noticing yourself having a new, mindful, and positive response in a situation that used to make you reactive feels so good. It's like a mini-enlightenment moment—one where you "wow" yourself. When the work you've been putting in actually *works* in life, it hits you that you've leveled up. And nothing gives you more motivation to keep going than seeing that type of effective growth happening in real time.

> **Reflecting on how much you've grown *proves* that you can change and have the *power* to shape your life in any way you imagine. All it takes is attention, effort, and patience.**

Use Bad Habits to Form Good Ones

After we become more aware of how we're moving through the world, we start receiving a lot of new information. We notice the positive ways we treat and speak to people. We notice how the work we've been putting in is translating into our lives and how much lighter we feel. Of course, everything has its balance. As we become more aware of the good, we also become more aware of the negative. We notice when we're feeling frustrated, selfish, or resentful. We see ourselves leaning in to judgment or allowing our anger or lack of patience to get the better of us.

Even though behaving in those ways is natural, it doesn't mean that it isn't embarrassing. When these behaviors arise, it can make us feel exposed. Imagining ourselves being reactive, sarcastic, or emotionally closed off in front of people we care about doesn't feel good. It's like watching an imaginary highlight reel of all our shortcomings in our head. Picturing this can make us feel frustrated and let down, like we'll never be able to grow past these negative behavior habits. It can also create anxiety because we worry about what else we're doing that we aren't aware of. We might ask ourselves:

- How could I have been doing this all along?
- Who have I acted this way toward without realizing it?
- Why do I *still* do this even though I'm aware of it?
- How can I move past this behavior pattern?

Becoming aware of your bad behavior or thinking habits can be a bummer. There have been plenty of times over the years that I've noticed my own patterns and wanted to crawl into a cave and hide for a couple of decades. But don't worry. Noticing them is a *good* thing. It's a huge breakthrough.

> **The hardest part of growth is becoming aware of the areas that need to grow.**

Think about the fact that you've been cruising through life on autopilot, doing whatever you do that makes your life worse without realizing it. For months, years, or even decades. Then one magical day, things line up, and a part of your awareness pings. You see yourself from the outside, and it clicks. Boom. You now have a new level of self-awareness that was *years* in the making. It's incredible that after so much time spent repeating the same patterns, you were able to change it. It's not something to beat yourself up over. It's something to celebrate.

Using Your Bad Habits as Reminders

It's useful to turn your bad habits into your employees. Put them to work and be a real uptight type of boss while you're at it. Instead of ignoring them when they appear, make them play a role in their own healing. See, a lot of times when we're flowing along in life, and we catch ourselves saying or doing something that doesn't feel aligned, we can easily turn a blind eye, feel bad for a minute, then continue with our day. That, of course, isn't a great way to operate because it doesn't solve anything. It just replants the seed of negativity and guarantees it will sprout again. Alternatively, when you notice yourself amid some kind of negative habit, you can use your awareness of it as a reminder to act in a new way. Here's how that can play out:

1. **Negative habit:** Let's say you notice you're not good at accepting compliments. When someone compliments you, you feel uncomfortable, guilty, and shy. You make a joke or try to brush off the compliment to get the attention off you.
2. **Positive retrain:** You receive a compliment and feel physical tension in your body rising. In this instance, you *notice* that this is happening. As you notice

yourself closing off, you use that negative feeling as a reminder to change your habits. So in the moment, you breathe, relax your muscles, open up, and allow yourself to receive the praise.

3. **Then, you speak thoughtfully:** You respond with a short and sweet "thank you" or "appreciate you" instead of a self-deprecating comment or distraction.

Using your negative habits as reminders to act in new ways like this is super helpful. What's great is that once you start practicing it a little, it becomes a trained reflex. Like, when you feel that negative, tense, toxic feeling in the pit of your stomach, you automatically know that you're playing out a bad habit and can push back against it by choosing to positively retrain it. Doing this is beautiful. It's like time travel in a strange way. It's allowing who you were in the past to help who you are in the present, and who you are in the present to help who you were in the past.

How to Stay Consistent on Your Path

So you've been watching your mind, staying present, and making intentional moves. You notice your life improving, your inner tension easing up, and your mental clarity increasing. It feels good. But after a little while, you notice that you're letting up on the effort and, in some cases, reverting to old patterns. Don't panic if—or I should say, when—this happens to you. And certainly, don't be hard on yourself about it. Everything goes through waves, phases, and cycles. Self-development is no different. That's why one of the most common questions people ask me is, "How can I stay consistent on my journey?"

Build It into Your Routine

> **We can't overcome the natural ebbs and flows of our effort, energy levels, and excitement. But we *can* strategize against them.**

Take those three things I listed at the start of this paragraph—the three E's—effort, energy, and excitement. When any one of those three things sags, we start to get out of the habit of living forward and start falling back into patterns of the past. We can protect ourselves from getting off track by ensuring we can continue our positive behaviors, even when we are running low on the three E's.

To stay consistent, we need to make our positive practices effortless, easy, and memorable. The best way to do that is to turn our practices into daily habits. Building new habits may seem complicated, but it is not. Where most people get it wrong is when they try to create a freestanding habit. That's when we decide to introduce some healthy practice into our lives and simply aim to "do it every day" without defining it further. While the intentions are good, seeking to achieve a goal this way is far too abstract. There's no commitment. No time, place, or incentive to achieve the goal. Essentially, we're just adding something else to our to-do list that can easily be put off and forgotten about.

However, habit stacking is a much more foolproof way to ensure consistency. This is when you add a new habit before or after a current habit to anchor it to an existing routine. Doing so shapes your new habit and helps you remember it by daisy-chaining it to something you already do.

For example, let's say you want to start meditating for 10 minutes every day. Instead of allowing the goal to float, where it is sure to take a back seat to other priorities, you'll want to add it to an existing sequence of daily events. In this instance, you could drop meditation into your morning preparation routine. Say you typically wake up, brush your teeth, exercise, shower, and drink coffee. You would want to place 10 minutes of meditation between showering and drinking coffee. By doing this, you are integrating meditation into an engrained sequence of events, making it automatic with minor repetitions. This may sound too simple to be true, but try it out. It works like a charm.

Mindful Consistency

We've just looked at how habit stacking is useful for something like meditation, a physical practice you want to introduce into your life. What's cool is that habit stacking also works when trying to build positive thinking habits. By keeping track of the habits in your speech, decision-making, and impulses, you can stack mindful habits with your existing ones to guide your overall behavior in healthy directions.

For example, say that you set a simple mindful goal, like being more open, kind, and comfortable with people you meet. After thinking about it, you decide you'll try to make your standard greetings a starting point of focus. That's a good thing to focus on because you can easily tune out when greeting strangers and be short or detached. Adding some warmth and presence can make a huge difference in the day of the person you're greeting and your day as well.

Here's how this looks in life: When you go to order your coffee from the barista, you might put your phone away and use that space to meet your goal by saying something warm, like you're talking to an old friend. When approaching the counter, you could pause, bring your awareness to the present moment for a few seconds, look at the barista as the deep, alive, feeling human that they are, connect with them with your eyes, and ask them from the heart, "How are you today?"

As simple and surface level as this might sound, you can feel the difference between transactional and connected human interactions.

> **While it may be a small gesture, sharing even a tiny present connection with others adds up and often means more to them than we realize.**

Brushing off or being cynical about small growth changes like this is tempting. However, making little changes like this reinforces a positive outlook, keeps you anchored to compassionate thinking, and helps you stay in the present moment. If you make a habit of inserting positive moments like these, they will eventually outnumber the neutral or negative moments you have, which will raise the overall positivity of your daily outlook.

Appreciate How Far You've Come

Once you get the hang of self-healing and personal growth, it becomes like a hobby. For one, it's fun because it gives you a project to work on. It's always entertaining because the project is you. And it's well worth the effort because, with each move you make, you feel lighter and brighter. You get a certain hunger for positive change, and by sticking to it for a while, your progress picks up momentum. This forward-flowing force keeps you looking into the future, always thinking about how you might next clarify, expand, and evolve yourself.

After getting into a positive flow like this, it's wise to remember to pause every now and then and reflect on how far you've come. Doing this will keep you from getting burned out. Seeing how much you've changed for the better will give you confidence, fill you with gratitude, and inspire you to keep thriving.

Let's practice this right now to get a sense of how it feels. No matter how new you are to inner work, you're certain to be able to relate to this reflective thought practice:

Think about your past, then think about who you've become. Picture how you saw the world 5 or 10 years ago. Remember how your mind, decision-making, and confidence felt. Recall how impulsive your choices were and how much you felt like you were drifting compared to today.

You did that. You caused all that growth. It's easy to brush off compliments, chalk it up to the chance of life, or belittle your growth by comparing yourself to people who inspire you. The fact is that you are responsible for your personal evolution. You saw how you wanted your life to change, trusted your instincts, and worked to make it happen.

> **Remember this truth the next time you start doubting yourself. You've worked through tough times, overcome limits, and allowed yourself to be uncomfortable when you knew it'd help you grow. You've always figured out how to keep moving forward in the past, which means you'll continue to be able to figure things out in the future. Trust yourself. You'll keep getting it right.**

We're all too hard on ourselves sometimes and sell our achievements short. Reflecting on your past like this is helpful when feeling down or uninspired too. It's a good reminder that uses the cold, hard evidence of the past as a measuring stick to gauge how much better your life is in the present. I'd also say that reflecting on your growth is valuable when you're already feeling good. It's so easy to get used to what's "normal" and forget how far you've come. If you really dive into your perspective of the past, the present can blow your mind.

CHAPTER 12

THE WISDOM OF GOALS

I used to roll my eyes at the idea of setting goals. I'm not sure why, but for some reason, it just felt lame. I think on one hand, it seemed insulting, as if setting goals was admitting that I couldn't remember to do something that was supposed to be important to me. On the other hand, I think there was some resistance deep inside, a kind of fear that I couldn't achieve what I wanted. So if I set a goal, it would make my inability to achieve it clear to see. On top of that, setting goals felt kind of corny to me. Maybe it was just my inner all-black-wearing adolescent self still rebelling against structure, but that's how it felt.

So I spent years improvising professionally and personally. I accomplished many things, but it never felt like I was being as effective or clear as I wanted to be. I could easily knock out projects when I focused on them, but I was always frustrated that I never felt like I had a big-picture plan. If only there were a way to change that!

After reading a couple of business books, it occurred to me that perhaps it was time I set goals to try and achieve the outcomes that had been escaping me. To the surprise of no one, it worked. It's almost as if having a clear, defined, and concise destination to focus on makes you accountable and keeps you pointing in the right direction.

> **You can use goals for a variety of purposes. When people think about setting goals, they often think about professional metrics or financial goals. However, you can and should set goals for your inner-life practices as well.**

It may sound strange, but it's a helpful growth tool. In this chapter, we'll walk through what it looks like to set a goal for personal growth, how to follow through with it, and why it's beneficial.

Accomplishing inner-life goals is pretty straightforward. The problem is that most of us don't approach them like this. We overcomplicate things, spend energy in the wrong places, and then get burned out before getting anywhere. For the sake of clarity, let's survey how things usually go wrong when we feel called to make a personal change. After that, we'll look at how we might be able to do it better.

Generally, we get inspired by seeing someone else's evolution. That's good energy, because watching someone we know or follow on social media grow demonstrates that change is possible. However, in these moments of peak inspiration, we have a hard time managing our enthusiasm. So we set unrealistic goals, and then when our initial enthusiasm wears off, we lose steam and then lose interest.

For example, say you listened to someone on a podcast talking about meditation. During the episode, the person interviewed shares that they've been meditating for over 20 years. They list incredible benefits such as lower anxiety, a clearer mind, more compassion, and greater self-insight. You hear this interview at just the right time, and it unlocks something inside you. That day, you decide to get some of that into your life. So you decide to start meditating for an hour in the morning and evening.

The first day of your new meditation schedule is easy because the inspiration from the day before is still with you. As the days pass, your energy decreases, and you find it harder to meet your goal. You make excuses about why you must cut back your meditation to only an hour in the morning. Then, you begin to feel you aren't doing well at meditation, which gives the whole experience a vibe of disappointment. That feeling lingers, and eventually you phase out meditating altogether.

This cycle is as old as time. We get so pumped when that key in us turns and unlocks the feeling of new possibilities. Then, we try way too hard, way too fast, with too little clarity and end up working against ourselves. That's why setting clear and *attainable* goals is the key to keeping yourself on track and energized for the long haul.

How to Set Attainable Goals

One of the common problems people have with achieving their goals is confusing a general desire to improve their lives with a precise way to do so. For example, you could notice that your stress levels have been much higher recently. So you decide to slow down and practice self-care more regularly. While this is a good intention to have, it's broad and leaves a lot of room for uncertainty and drifting.

Make Your Goal Clear

When you approach "lowering your stress," you might drink water instead of alcohol one night. Then, the next night, you put your phone away for two hours before bed. On day three, you meditate in the morning. Doing all these things is a great start, but the problem is that after a week or so, you'll start hitting an energy barrier. When you run out of random self-care practices, you'll then have to use mental energy to research, learn, and plan new ways to de-stress yourself, and you know what that does. Causes stress. So you start dropping the new positive habits you're trying to build and go back to cuddling up in bed with a bottle of wine and a glowing screen.

> **Making your goal clear is crucial because that makes it defined, trackable, and apparent.**

Instead of drifting through a buffet of self-care rituals, you would want to choose one and stick to it for a decent period of time. That way, you feel the benefits of the practice and have a single, defined thing to do each day with no resistance.

An example of making a clear goal could be, "I will only drink alcohol one day this week." Doing this creates a clear metric to follow, stick to, and feel progress over time. After sticking with that well-defined goal for a week or two, you will be able to feel that you've gotten better sleep, you're rehydrated, and your nervous system has cooled off. By doing this, you will have successfully reduced your stress levels and given yourself a chance to rebalance.

Make Your Goal Realistic

An important part of making your goals successful is making them attainable. As we discussed a few pages ago, getting lost in your enthusiasm and setting the bar too high almost always backfires. While it might seem appealing at first, your energy is sure to deplete over time, which makes it hard to keep up the pace you had at the outset. When you start missing your goals, you feel bummed, like you're failing, and your motivation plummets. You don't want that. You want the opposite of that. So you should work in the opposite way. Setting an *attainable* goal allows you to hit it, even when you're feeling tired or uninspired. Doing this builds your energy, gives you an emotional boost because you feel like you accomplished something, and creates stable motivation.

> **When we hit our goal, we feel good about ourselves. And guess what? We like feeling good about ourselves. So reaching our realistic goal each day**

becomes something we *crave* instead of something we *resist*.

In only a few weeks of practice, our brains' neuroplasticity rewires, and we begin to *desire* reaching our goal on a biological level. This change happens because when we feel good about ourselves, our brains release "feel-good" hormones like dopamine, serotonin, and endorphins.

Since reaching our attainable goal creates a biological reward, we become driven *from the inside out* to meet it every day. This change reshapes our motivation from extrinsic (seeking an outside reward or approval) to intrinsic (seeking an internal reward or self-approval). Once we establish our motivation in this way, hitting our goal each day becomes effortless. That's because it becomes something *we enjoy* rather than a chore to cross off our endless to-do list.

Manage Your Energy

I've mentioned the importance of managing your energy a few times. That's because it's a crucial part of personal growth and often overlooked. Many people end up thinking the reason they aren't reaching their self-growth goals is that they aren't capable or don't have the skill. That's not true. In most cases, it's a simple case of not knowing how to properly manage energy. Let's walk through the process of getting inspired, taking action, and managing energy so we can see what this looks like in life.

There's always an impetus that sends us off in a new and inspired direction. In almost every case, that motivation starts externally. For example, we could hear someone share their journey on a podcast, read a self-help book, or see a friend flourishing on their growth path. However it comes about, the key is to be *in the right headspace* and ready to seek change. Then, we need to *receive new information* that ties together several ideas that have been lingering in our minds for a while.

When this happens, we have what's called an *insight*. Having an insight is when deep intuitive clarity hits us. This understanding can be about ourselves, others, a situation, or a creative solution. Insights are powerful. They are genuine moments of clarity where our perception shifts and we gain new perspectives. When insights happen, they are almost always accompanied by a surge of energy. We get this blast of energy because we've spent time weighed down by something inside us that we couldn't figure out how to resolve. When the insight hits, we can see the solution and learn how to move forward on our path. This understanding evaporates the feeling of heaviness that we've been carrying. However, the resistance we've been applying to our heaviness remains, so when the blockage moves, we intensely explode forward.

Since these moments are rare, we don't have much experience with them. This unfamiliarity makes it challenging to know what to do with all the energy we have received. So we typically blow our energy too fast, get burned out, and can't reach our goal.

For example, our bodies could feel tense, inflexible, and sore. Then, we hear someone talk about yoga in a way that addresses all of the pain points we are looking to heal. Imagining feeling flexible, open, and free of body pain excites us to heal our bodies. With all this energy running through us, we start doing yoga for an hour a day. We might keep this up for a week, but our initial energy will eventually fade. Then, it will become progressively harder to meet our one-hour yoga goal. As this happens, we start getting more burned out. As time passes, we start looking at yoga as a chore.

An outcome like this is extremely common. It's also why clarifying the goal is essential. If we recall from earlier, the initial goal was not to "do an hour of yoga a day." It was to relieve physical tension, become flexible, and reduce body aches. However, we mismanaged our energy and allowed our enthusiasm to make us lose sight of the big picture.

> **An intellectually mature way to approach what we want to achieve is to make a clear goal, then spend the blast of energy we received from our insight patiently over time.**

Otherwise, it's like we're getting our paycheck on the first of the month and blowing all our cash in the first week. Then, we get to treat ourselves to eating dry ramen packets for the next three weeks. On the other hand, say you get your paycheck on the first of the month and budget responsibly. By doing that, you can eat well throughout the month and avoid drying up like a beached jellyfish from slurping all of that sodium.

Continuing with the yoga example, let's look at how you can achieve your goal while appropriately managing your energy. A balanced approach would be to consider the goal (relieve tension, increase flexibility) and how much energy you'll need to spend to achieve it. In this case, you could start with a test schedule of doing yoga for 30 minutes every other day. After practicing this for a week, you would want to check in with yourself to see how things are going.

Ask yourself clarifying questions like: Am I getting the results I desire? Is my enthusiasm for doing yoga going up, down, or sustaining? Depending on the answers to these questions, you can adjust your schedule to increase or decrease the frequency you practice yoga. Doing this will help you approach your goal in an intelligent, balanced, and healthy way, keeping you from burning out and massively improving your chances for sustainable growth.

Hold Yourself Accountable

Accountability is a powerful force. Imagine that you're trying to run a mile at a fast pace. Then, imagine you're trying to run a mile with a friend waiting at the finish line with a stopwatch. You're definitely going to pick up the pace when your friend is timing you because they are holding you accountable. The reality is that few of us push ourselves if no one is watching. Lack of accountability is why most people give up on their inner growth. When trying to reach a personal goal, no one is there to push you to succeed.

> ***You have to be the one* to motivate yourself, not let yourself off the hook, and choose to gut it out and keep pushing when resistance is high.**

Doing this may sound hard, but it isn't. It's just about sticking with it, keeping your eye on the prize, and remembering that big moves are built with small steps.

Track your progress. Slow changes take time to see. Those micro-shifts seem invisible when you're working on something every day. The reality is that compounding those small changes is how you get significant results. Yet, since we can't detect changes on a daily basis, it's easy to get discouraged and lose inspiration. For example, if we decide to get in better shape, we can shift our lifestyle habits. We could focus on eating healthier, exercising daily, taking supplements, and staying hydrated. However, even though we're doing the work for days or weeks, we might not see any visible results when we look in the mirror.

Experiencing this can be disheartening because we *know* we're putting in the work, but still, it doesn't feel like that work is paying off. The truth is that getting in shape takes time. That's why it's referred to as a lifestyle change. It's a marathon, not a sprint. A person working toward better physical shape and doing everything right can only expect to lose about a pound a week. Now, if you spend five days a week sweating it out in the gym, you will expect serious results after a month. But the truth is, at best, you'll only drop about five pounds in that time. This messes with our heads. It makes it feel like our effort isn't worth it and is usually why people stop working toward their goals.

However, if you track your progress, things take a different shape. If you're working hard in the gym and eating well, you might not see any visible changes in the mirror. But if you consistently weigh yourself first thing in the morning before having any fluids or food, you can observe the micro-changes in real time. You'll see that you don't look any different now but have lost five pounds over the past four weeks. Seeing that kind of trackable progress makes imperceivable change perceivable. Your inspiration remains invigorated by seeing that you're getting somewhere. You keep from thinking yourself into giving up, and you can keep moving forward toward your goal with confidence.

Tracking inner-life goals can be approached in the same way. Doing this may seem tricky because internal changes occur in the mind. However, it's easy to create systems that track internal progress. The key is keeping an objective journal or log of behaviors. In other words, you want to write down your growth habits on paper or on your phone. They need to live outside of your head. That's because if we try to remember our progress, it will eventually melt together, become unclear, and be hard to quantify.

Let's look at how we might track our inner goals:

Say you decide to communicate more thoughtfully.

Draw a box on a piece of paper or create a notepad document on your phone that represents your current week. Write the date beside it so the week will be clear.

From there, watch for moments where you notice yourself making space for others, listening deeply, or speaking with intention.

When you notice this, make a mark in the box or put an X on the note on your phone. Then, when you look back at your document, you can see how many times you communicated mindfully for that week.

Suppose you notice that the number was low or not progressing from the previous week. In that case, you have precise data that shows you need to put more effort into practicing mindful communication. You can quit tracking data once you feel satisfied with your progress. At this point, the pattern will have grown into a consistent behavioral habit, and you won't need to put in the intentional effort, as the action will have become ingrained in who you are.

Rest Is Growth

I know we've been talking about growth, progress, and goals for a while now, so I want to take a break from that and talk about something just as important as leveling up our lives. Taking time off.

> **We have a hard time remembering that rest is an essential part of the inner-growth path.**

It should be no surprise, either. Looking at culture, we see people grinding away, posting their achievements, and living a life of endless, seamless accomplishments. That is because, from the start, social media trained us to show only the moments of our lives that stoke desire in others. This taught an entire generation that looking good to others is what's most important. It also had the unsurprising side effect of making people believe the 24/7 hustle is a reality, which caused real pressure and a deep fear of failure. As culture normalized those feelings, a large majority of people started living in 24/7 grind mode because they thought that's what life was supposed to be.

Fortunately, the spell of the never-ending grind is starting to break. You can see a counterculture on social media calling for people to slow down, create space in their lives, and focus more on *being* rather than *doing*. I'm grateful this evolution is taking place, as it's essential to our cultural health. Learning to take rest seriously is a major part of the journey. We have to know that.

> **Rest isn't just about restoring your energy. It's also about giving yourself enough space to reflect so you can strengthen your perspective.**

Taking time off from trying to grow gives us time to live at a different frequency for a while. In this space, we can integrate our changes, reconnect with ourselves, and regain our footing on the path. Doing this helps us understand where we are in our lives. And understanding where we are is crucial because it's the only way to know where to go next.

Ultimately, we should flip our perspective on what rest is. We often think about it as periods of being "lazy" or "not accomplishing anything." That couldn't be further from the truth.

> ***Rest is growth.* Taking time to recharge is essential because when we spend energy, we aren't growing; we're pushing boundaries and increasing our capacity for change. Rest is when we stop moving and grow into the new space we've created.**

Don't pressure yourself into a nonstop grind of trying to grow and achieve. Know that these things are seasonal. There's no reason to feel guilty for taking time off. It's something to be proud of because you know how to see the big picture and maturely respect yourself. Listen to how you feel. Give yourself time to rest, integrate, and self-reflect. Then, when the time is right, you'll know you're ready to bloom again.

CHAPTER 13

MAKE REAL PROGRESS

How often have you worked hard to make personal change, only to look up a few weeks or months later and realize that you haven't gotten anywhere? That feeling is the worst. It makes you feel frustrated and deflated, and it keeps you from *believing* that you can make the changes in your life that you want to. For some, this feeling can be a nasty moment. Slowly over time, you can get into the habit of believing that you aren't capable and lose your feeling of personal power.

Don't worry if you feel a little helpless, stuck, or unable to make real progress. It's all good. You aren't alone. I've had an endless stream of people reach out to me and share that they feel this way. It doesn't mean anything is wrong with you. It probably just means that you need to shift your perception and change the way you work toward making personal progress. In this chapter, we're going to refresh the way we think about progress, effort, and timing so we can get a stable path of inner growth under our feet.

The Progress Illusion

One of the key things that keep people from progressing on their personal goals is misperception. That means that how you think about the action you're taking, the effort you're putting in, and the results you should be seeing isn't informed or realistic. To change that, you want to close the gap between reality and your perception of reality. I like to call this problem the *progress illusion*. This happens when we mistake *thinking* about change with actually *taking action*.

To explain how this goes down, I'm going to use learning how to meditate as an example. At some point, inspiration strikes you. You're watching a documentary, listening to a podcast, or reading a book, and it hits you that you should finally learn how to meditate. And this time, you mean it. Realistically, when the thought enters your mind, "Hey, I'm going to learn to meditate," you don't drop everything, rush over to your phone, and start learning. There's a marination period. You take a little time to sit with the inspiration and figure out how you want to try to learn. You roll it over in your head. Do you want to use an app? Take an in-person class? Learn from a friend?

You also spend some time daydreaming about what it would be like if you became a great meditator. You imagine having a clear mind, feeling calm, and radiating a profound sense of presence for everyone else to enjoy. After spending a week or so with this idea, you eventually decide to use an app to learn some meditation basics. So you download the app of your choice and load up the first lesson. You then spend about 10 minutes working with the app, learning how to use it, and getting started with the entry-level lesson. Then, the next day, you remember your desire to learn meditation, bust out the app, and work with it for another 10 minutes. On day three, you have a busy day and forget to do another lesson.

You drive past a yoga studio a week later and remember your meditation app. So the next day, you open up the app and work with it for another 10 minutes. Things get busy again, so you forget the app, and this time you forget about it for three days. Then, you're listening to a podcast, and someone mentions meditation, and you remember, "Oh yeah, I forgot to practice again." Now you start feeling a little frustrated. I mean, you've been working toward learning to meditate for weeks, and you still have no clue how to levitate, transcend this dimension of reality, or comprehend the meaning of the universe.

While feeling a little frustration at that moment is understandable, what's true is that two narratives are at play. Let's zoom out and take a broader look at what happened throughout this story.

You spent several weeks *thinking* about learning to meditate. However, you only opened the app and put in 30 minutes of real effort. This is where the progress illusion kicks in. In this example, you spent several weeks with the idea that you were going to learn to meditate, so it *feels* like you are putting in work. But the reality is that, in the story, you are confusing the *idea* of putting in work with actually working toward your goal.

> **Learning to watch for this is helpful because it keeps you realistic in your expectations, clear about where you should be in your progress, and free from beating yourself up when you aren't as far along as you hoped you'd be.**

Imagine how many times you've gone through this cycle of events without realizing it. I know I certainly have. The fact that concepts can sit on the hard drive of our mind in a strangely visible, yet passive position makes it so easy to feel like we're "working really hard" on something whenever we've hardly applied ourselves at all. Throughout the rest of this chapter, we'll try to put an end to the progress illusion by exploring a model of change that will illuminate some useful self-understanding.

The Stages of Change Model

In the 1970s, researchers James Prochaska and Carlo DiClemente developed the transtheoretical model of behavior change, also called the stages of change model, because they were interested in helping people make more effective changes in their lives. The two professors applied the model to everything from smoking cessation and depression reduction to stress management and more. There has been a robust amount of research on the model's use, which has determined it is an effective method for change and habit intervention. The model breaks down the stages of change into five distinct parts. It begins with the stage where a person is entirely *unaware* that they need to make a change and goes to the final stage of maintenance mode. I've applied a version of this model here to broaden our perspective and help us think differently about personal change.

The stages of change model is useful because it's rooted in awareness and clearly defines the steps to take to make meaningful change. Most of the time, we get off track when we are trying to improve a certain part of our lives because the whole process is so unclear. Our attention and focus drift, we lose track of where we are in the process, and eventually we get distracted and stop trying to move forward. Being able to have some clear self-guidance helps us understand where we are, what to do next, and how our progress is going.

Here are brief descriptions of the five stages of change:

1. **Precontemplation.** At this stage, we still need to become aware that a change is needed. We're living on autopilot and probably feeling confused about why we're unhappy. We often know that we don't feel great but haven't made the connection to what's causing it or what change we could make to improve things.

   For example, you could be sleeping poorly and have trouble focusing in the afternoon. However, you've yet to make the connection that it's because you've gotten into the habit of having three drinks at night. In this case, your symptoms will continue until you are aware of which actions are causing them.

2. **Contemplation.** Here we have become aware that we need to make a change. It doesn't mean that we have actively started taking steps to make that change. We've just started thinking about change

because we had an insight. The likely case is that we made a connection between our behavior and a new desired outcome. So that concept is now in our heads as a potential action we can take to reduce our negative feelings.

Following our example, we would *become aware* that having three drinks a night disrupts our sleep and makes us feel hazy in the morning. After realizing this, we would think, "I should drink less to feel better." However, we still haven't taken any action.

3. **Preparation.** Now that we know what change we want to make, we move to the preparation stage. At this point, we start gathering information, acquiring whatever tools we may need, and preparing our daily routines for integration. In terms of our example, we might read about how alcohol affects sleep, make our alcohol bottles less readily accessible, and come up with a healthy limit of drinks a week to stick to.
4. **Action.** Finally, we reach the second-to-last stage where we begin taking action. Here we use our awareness of the change we want to make as motivation and follow through with the plan we came up with during the preparation stage. Since our example goal is getting better sleep and feeling more clearheaded during the day, we decide to limit our alcohol intake. Say we devised a plan to have no drinks during the week, then two a day on the weekends. We follow that regime and stick to it until we get positive results.
5. **Maintenance.** After we've started taking action, made our change, and are seeing results, we enter an important and often overlooked stage. When we reach a goal, we tend to feel like we no longer have to work at it. That's because we feel like we're "done," as if we've reached a finish line and things will take care

of themselves now. Not true. Once we make a change, we don't have to put in the same effort we did to get there. However, it's important to *maintain* our behavior change with regular effort. Doing this is how we integrate the new change into our lives so it becomes a permanent habit rather than a momentary diversion.

Finishing up with our example, we can become more flexible with how many drinks we have on any evening. However, to maintain the change, we wouldn't revert to our previous behavior of having three beverages a night. We would continue to consciously limit our intake while allowing the patterns to breathe more than we did under the strict rule that helped us reach our goal and strengthen our mental clarity.

Gaining Clarity on Your Path

After looking at the stages of change model, I suggest that you consider where it is that you normally get stuck. Thinking about this is useful because it gives insight into your own patterns, helps raise self-awareness, and keeps you from falling prey to the same predators of progress. From what I can tell—given the feedback I hear—the majority of people get caught in the *contemplation stage*. That makes sense because we all live in our heads so much.

> **Our imaginations often feel like reality. One of the many problems this creates is that we mistake our imagination *for* reality. So as we go through life thinking about the changes we want to make, it's so easy, almost natural for us, to confuse thinking about taking action with actually doing so.**

Being real with yourself and tracking your effort is a great way to ensure you don't get stuck in the contemplation stage. For example, to work meditation into your daily routine, try throwing it on your phone calendar with a reminder notification. Nothing too fancy. Simply put the word *Meditate* as the title and have it repeat at the same time every day. That way, you'll have an outside force reminding you to practice meditation, and it will be crystal clear when you *decide* to skip a day for some reason. Not only will this help you stay consistent, but it will also help you stay realistic with yourself about how much effort you're putting in. That's super valuable because, in the long run, knowing *exactly* how much time you've spent on the cushion will properly manage your expectations. It will also keep you from believing you should be further along in your levels of mastery than you are, which can cause frustration and a lack of motivation.

Regardless of the area of your inner life you're looking to improve at any given point in time, self-auditing, setting clear goals, and sticking to a plan is a surefire way to help you make real progress. So many people have a deep desire to grow but get off track when the path starts feeling blurry. If this happens to you, make this objective way of monitoring your progress a lifeline that you can hold on to when you start feeling like you're treading water.

Even if you discover that you haven't been putting in as much work as you thought, that's okay. As long as it reminds you that you *are* capable, and by working at your own pace and keeping track of your progress, you can unquestionably lift up your life the way you hope possible.

PART IV

LET GO, FIND PEACE

CHAPTER 14

IF YOU WANT TO BE HELPFUL, HELP YOURSELF

We all start focusing on self-healing for different reasons. That is to say, because we live unique lives, our mental pain emerges in different ways. Many of us had rough childhoods that inflicted deep wounds. We then carry those wounds with us into adulthood until we begin to realize that the way they make us feel needs to be healed.

> **Carrying pain inside of us for a long time, especially during our early years, greatly impacts how we see the world.**

Oddly enough, living with pain can make us more sensitive and colder at the same time. We're more sensitive because we can resonate with the pain of others since we've been forced to feel the same thing. It gives us a direct experience of how terrible inner heaviness can feel. So when we see someone else going through it, we know exactly what they're feeling. This type of insight can make us more empathetic and allow us to show up for those in pain in profound ways.

On the other hand, living with suffering can make us turn off our emotions too. When we're feeling emotionally exhausted, we may have nothing left to give other people because we're worn down from dealing with our own pain. Sometimes this makes it hard to be empathetic to people who could use support. Going deeper, there are times when we are drained, hear someone struggling, and get irritated at how surface level their troubles seem compared to what we're feeling. When this happens, we're likely to become distant and close off our flow of compassion.

Living with this kind of heavy emotional burden weighs us down. We have to force our way through our lives, battling our feelings about ourselves and the difficulties our emotions create in our relationships. At some point, the heaviness of what we carry becomes too much. Regardless of how, where, when, or why we feel the way we do, we *begin to realize* that, going forward, the way we feel isn't sustainable. This is a big moment. It's one that unifies us all, regardless of what kind of wounds we carry.

Experiencing this is a moment of self-awareness.

Eventually, our suffering becomes too much. We get frustrated enough by it to hit a tipping point, or we have an experience with someone else that reflects our pain to us. When this happens, we see our pain from a new perspective. It then becomes clear that what we consistently feel isn't "normal." In most cases, since inner wounds happen when we are young, we grow up thinking it's how things are because we don't have a frame of reference for feeling any other way. Having this insight that there is a way through this suffering and that we *no longer have to live with it* is super motivating.

During this time, our inspiration drives us to start looking for teachings, methods, techniques, books—anything that could help us heal. As we start integrating healing practices, understanding our pain more clearly, and letting go of what's holding us down, we often can't help but share our experiences with others. This is common because when we start feeling lighter, we want to shout it from the top of a mountain. We have new life breathing inside of us and want anyone who might be suffering in the same way to hear that a new life is possible. I can vouch for the fact that this is true. I started a podcast about it and made it my life's work.

While sharing our personal journeys is an important and useful thing to do, there are also pitfalls to watch for at this stage of the path. In this chapter, we're going to take a look at many ways that we can end up doing ourselves a disservice while we're trying to be of service to others.

The Habit of Healing Others

Once we get on the path to growth, it typically takes up a lot of space in our lives. That makes sense, of course, because our *suffering* takes up so much space in our lives. If we're going to be working on that, we will need to spend a lot of time thinking, researching, and talking about it. So we dedicate a lot of our time to working on ourselves, and it sort of becomes who we are.

Interestingly, when people start doing the work, their personalities tend to undergo noticeable shifts. Sometimes friends or family members can react to this change in a negative way because, to them, it seems like your identity isn't stable. That makes them uncomfortable. They may think you've changed. And it's like, yeah, that's what I've been going for!

> **Identity changes start taking place because *you* are changing. As you change your thinking habits, work through pain, and take a new approach to life, you're going to start feeling and acting differently. This is a *good* thing.**

It means you're breaking the mold of your old patterns, feeling more alive, and taking charge of your happiness. Almost like clockwork, there is a time in the early stages of your journey when you feel full of energy, optimistic, and radiate positive energy. This is when you have put in enough work to offload some heaviness and feel like you're floating. It's a beautiful time on the path, but there are some things to be mindful of.

Comparison

Once we've begun feeling and thinking in fresh ways, we enter unknown territory in our lives. We spent the first several decades with one view of the world and ourselves, and now, over the course of a few months, our perceptions and emotions have shifted. Think of it as a new mental landscape. And like in any new landscape, there are new obstacles to watch out for.

Awareness is what kick-starts our journey toward a better life. Becoming aware of our suffering makes us aware of the negative ways our pain has caused us to think and act. Now, once it expands, this kind of awareness isn't limited to just us. Once we see something within ourselves, we can start to see it everywhere. That means that as we grow, we begin to recognize our own negative behaviors in other people.

It may come as a surprise, but when we recognize suffering in others, it can have a nasty way of turning into frustration and judgment. When *we know* the steps a friend or family member can take to help heal themselves, but they aren't taking them, it can make us irritated and angry. Our emotions come from a good place. We see that this person is suffering and want to help them, yet they won't take the initiative and help themselves. The longer we watch them in pain without taking action, the more frustrated we feel. Eventually, our perception of that person can shift. Without intending to do so, we may start to judge these types of people for not helping themselves, even though we've tried to help them. Doing this can cause cracks in relationships and loosen what could have once been tight connections.

In situations like these, it's important to remember that the reason a person can't take any steps forward is that they have yet to become *aware* of their circumstances. When feeling frustrated that someone isn't taking charge of their lives, it can be useful to remember back to before *we* had our initial insight of self-awareness. We were just like them. Going through life in a prolonged state of pain, mindlessly accepting that how we felt was how things are.

Not everyone is on the same timeline. Each person's path emerges in its own way in its own time. Neither you nor they can force it, because moments of insight are spontaneous. They happen while the person is in the appropriate emotional and intellectual state of mind. Then, the right series of events have to take place to trigger the insight. It may be challenging to watch a friend or family member wrestle with their pain while unable to see themselves.

Naturally, we want to help in those times because we know how they are feeling and how they might be able to grow. But it's wise to remember that we can't force them to do so. We can only be patient with them while they are on their way. Doing this will keep you from getting frustrated with people you care about and possibly looking at them in a negative light.

> **You can't make anyone else change. But what you can do is *support* them. Talk with people in this situation about what they're feeling, offer them some of the same tools you've used, and be ready to listen when they need an open ear.**

Converting

It's hard not to talk about it when we make progress on our path and our worlds start changing from the inside out. Because we are in the driver's seat of our experience and have started feeling *so much better,* we have an intimate, firsthand knowledge of just how revitalizing personal growth can be. Feeling this new surge of life inside of us is almost bedazzling. It perks up our senses, gives us a feeling that the universe is at our backs, pushing us forward, and that our future has endless possibilities. This blast of life force that enters people who are putting in the work is quite real and easy to see. It's what makes people radiant and lets them emanate the sensation of presence.

As we go through these changes ourselves and begin feeling this way, we start to get somewhat possessed by the ecstatic nature of the energy. It compels us to make new choices, disrupt our past behavior patterns, and share our feelings with everyone around us. Wanting to share the energy we feel is a great thing. It comes from a good place too. After feeling so heavy for so long, we finally feel full of life again and want everyone we care about to feel the same.

Many people in your life *love* feeling the energy coming off you. In some ways, you become a beacon of goodness they can count on and gain inspiration from. That's all good. However, what I've noticed is people filled with new energy often try to convince people *who aren't interested in change* to follow the path that they have followed. Again, the impulse comes from a good place, but that doesn't mean it won't cause problems.

For example, if you travel to be with your family for the holidays, you'll likely see people you haven't seen for a while. Since you've been putting in the work and are full of new energy, you have the instinct to share your story with them in the hopes that they can experience some of the wonderful changes that you have. However, they might not be interested or ready for personal change at that point in time. So a situation emerges where you are trying to *convert* them to your form of inner growth.

No matter how great we feel, we can't convince other people in our lives to follow the same path we have. As mentioned earlier, it could be that they aren't ready, and it could also be that they simply don't care. Most people aren't seeking personal growth. They're trying to get by, ignore their inner lives, and get on with it. That, of course, is fine for them—it's where they're at right now. But, for example, it's not great if you're at the dinner table *pressuring* people to engage with you about your transformation.

To you, it feels like you're offering valuable wisdom to people you care about. But to them, you might as well be trying to convince them about the beautiful and empowering benefits of learning to speak Icelandic. It's important to remember that sometimes other people simply have no frame of reference or real interest in what you're trying to share with them.

So if you try to convince people you care about to make personal changes who aren't interested, they might react in negative ways. For one, they can feel like you're judging them by assessing where they are at and determining that they need to work on themselves. People can also get frustrated because they don't understand what you're talking about. That can make a person feel dumb, which in turn makes them feel angry. Telling people that they should grow can also make them feel like you're questioning how they've chosen to live their lives, which can make them feel offended. In turn, you can become frustrated because you feel like you're sharing from the heart and aren't being heard.

When you're in the early stages of growth and are feeling filled with energy, it's wise to play it cool, be respectful, and worry about yourself instead of trying to force your story on other people. If you spend enough time around people that you hope will grow, they might notice that you have an energy that shows you're living lighter. When someone notices this on their own, instead of being told to, they typically become curious. They'll want to get some of that feeling in their lives and will ask you how.

> **Once they have opened the door on their own, you can start bringing your wisdom into their lives.**

Be Your Change

At this point, you might be thinking, "So . . . is there no way I can help people I care about?" Don't worry. There is, and really, all it takes is a little patience. Live as an example. I know that may sound like a cliché. But it's a deep one.

See, everyone is always at different places on their journeys. Some people haven't started at all, and others are further along than us. Whatever the case, human motivation simply doesn't work from the outside. It has to come from the inside out. You can't force someone to understand something that you understand. The other person has to want to seek change themselves, be hungry for growth, and start walking on their path using their own two feet.

So the best way—really the only way—to help other people is to help yourself. By being consistent, working with tough emotions, letting go, becoming vulnerable, and embracing your power, you will level up your life in unbelievable ways. What's wild is that once you follow your path long enough, you start to feel like you're living in a new timeline. Reflecting on how reactive you were, how cloudy your mind was, and how emotionally immature you were is mind-blowing. It doesn't even feel like you could have been that person at one point in your life. A useful insight is that if you think about it, many people who you care about *currently* perceive the world how you *used to.*

Remembering this is incredibly valuable. Once we grow, we get used to who we've become, and many of the ideas that were once transformative for us now feel like common sense. So that can make them feel apparent to us, making it easy for us to forget that other people might not understand these things in the way we do. And if you reflect on how you saw the world before you started growing, you can probably see looking back that what people said to you didn't get through. It was what you *saw* in people that did. Again, this is effective because what people say to us hits us from the outside. But when *we* recognize something on our own, the insight grows from inside of us and feels intimate.

> **This is why your best act of service is treating yourself well, continuing on your path, and living as an example of integrity. The more your cup fills, the more it will overflow.**

People around you will notice the way you handle situations, the insightful comments you make, and the present feeling that comes from you. They will sense your self-awareness and ability to think with a stunning clarity. In their own time, when what needs to align for them aligns, you will—through simply being the best you—be a source of inspiration for them. A true, shining example that change and growth are possible. In the meantime, all you have to do is be patient and live up to your standards. Then, when they ask, be ready to share your map so they can find the beginning of their own path.

Allow Yourself to Accept Your Own Love

Many of us come to the path of personal growth because we have painful backgrounds. Because of this, it's common for us to avoid or feel guilty about treating ourselves well. Spending years feeling hurt, broken, and down on ourselves can train us to believe that we don't deserve to feel whole. When this happens, people who become self-aware about their suffering will gently work on themselves but often spend far more energy trying to help others. This behavior comes from a place of guilt and a feeling of unworthiness.

Feeling unloved by family members, betrayed by a partner, or stricken with personal tragedy can make us feel like there's a cosmic reason we're suffering. We get that feeling because pain like this hits us on such a deep level that it can't be intellectually processed. It goes against logic. It feels embedded in life, which makes us feel like there's something wrong with us or that we have to live with the pain we were dealt. These feelings make us outwardly focused. Sometimes we can find ourselves trying to grow simply so we don't inconvenience others with our pain.

We can spend much of our time learning how to be there for others, broadening our emotional horizons, and cultivating our mental clarity without ever really feeling better. Living like this gives us the illusion that we're giving ourselves love and healing when really, we're just ignoring the core of what's causing our suffering.

Be sure you aren't helping others while avoiding taking care of yourself. If you're doing this, it can feel like you're getting somewhere on your path, and you are in a way, but you're also leaving a huge part of yourself behind.

> **You have to stake a claim to your own health, happiness, and emotional freedom. You are worth it, and it's okay to give yourself love and care. It isn't selfish, and there's no reason for you to feel guilty for treating yourself well. Just because other people in your life didn't know how to love you properly doesn't mean that you aren't worthy of proper love.**

Learning to accept your own love is a process. It's a skill, and like any skill, it takes time to figure out how to do it in a way that feels good to you. Here are a few ways that you can start to show yourself the love you deserve:

1. Make space to take care of your body and mind.

When we don't feel worthy of feeling good, we neglect our physical and mental health. Make it a priority to eat well, sleep well, and do things *you* enjoy, which positively affects your mental health.

2. Create emotional boundaries.

You don't have to sink all your emotional energy into other people. Create proper boundaries with people so you don't have to spend energy if you don't feel up to it. Emotional offerings are something you *give* to others. Like all gifts, they shouldn't be expected. And you shouldn't give them if you can't afford them. If you're feeling drained or low, take time for yourself and save your emotional energy.

3. Do things just for you.

When we don't feel worthy of love, we have a hard time doing things just for us. That's because we don't feel like we are worth it.

Break that habit by taking time at least once a week to do something for *you* that makes you happy.

4. Ask for help when you need it.

Many people who have difficulty showing themselves love also have a problem asking for help. Feeling like you aren't worthy of help makes you grind everything out in life, even when you could use some support. Make it a habit to talk to your friends when you need advice or help. No one can handle life by themselves. And going to a friend for help is not only useful, it also has the beautiful byproduct of deepening personal bonds.

Doing any of these things can be hard at first. I know firsthand. But you really have to sit down with yourself and think: "You know what? I'm tired of letting pain from the past rule how I feel in the present. I'm tired of not giving myself the love I deserve. I'm over feeling depleted and sucked dry. I will claim my space in life and show myself love because I'm worth it like anyone else."

Having a chat like this with yourself is a *mindset shift*. It's when you are self-aware in the present, and you *choose* to start thinking and acting differently. When you start showing yourself love, you might feel self-conscious or shy about it at first. But keep going.

> **Keep believing and trusting that you're worth it. Once you start feeling how good it feels to feel full, you'll never settle for feeling empty again.**

CHAPTER 15

CONNECT TO YOURSELF WITH STILLNESS

When was the last time you sat and did nothing? I'm not talking about sitting on the couch with your phone. I mean sitting without any input at all while letting your mind open and your body decompress. If you're like most people, then it's probably been a while. We all struggle with finding time to quiet our minds. It's wild how much there is to do in life to keep it all going, much less get ahead.

Even dealing with the logistics of being human—like constantly deciding what to eat, searching food out, then eating. Or bathing, doing laundry, cleaning your house, getting exercise, paying your bills, taking care of your pets, and maintaining some sliver of socialness, all while scheduling this around your work life. It's a lot. Sometimes I laugh to myself about going to the bathroom. It's a chore that never ends. You just have to keep going again and again.

Because the mere act of existing takes so much upkeep, our life gains a momentum of doing. By that, I mean that since there's always something we need to get done, we get into the habit of constantly doing stuff without ever taking a break to recover. Think of it like a train. Once it reaches its cruising speed, it takes a while to slow down. The train is too heavy and has too much momentum to stop on a dime. The conductor has to take time to slow down before the train can stop at the station. We operate in the same way, which is why we're so bad at slowing down and taking time for ourselves to simply *be*. We feel compelled to keep going because every task feels important because we have gotten into the habit of seeking important tasks.

> **Mindfully building time in your life to slow down is unbelievably valuable. Doing nothing other than being still and quiet for a few minutes a day gives your mind a break from the input. That break creates space in your thinking, allowing you to hear your own voice and get back in tune with your inner compass.**

By practicing being still consistently, you consciously turn the noise down in your life, which increases your mental clarity, energy levels, and motivation. The mindset shift stillness provides is a serious game changer.

Time after Time

Interestingly, if you ask most people—even those who fancy themselves high performers—if stillness is a powerful tool for personal transformation, they would say yes. However, these same people don't make time for stillness in their lives. Okay. So let's get this straight. We all *know* that being still for a few minutes a day is a huge boost to our happiness, yet we don't do it. Strange, isn't it? What makes it even more bizarre is that we all *yearn* for moments of relaxation and decompression. People spend months daydreaming about going on vacation so they can let go, step out of the momentum of their lives, and reconnect with themselves.

Yet what they are looking for is available to them every day, and they pass it up.

So why do we ignore practicing stillness even though we know it will make our lives better?

> **We've been conditioned to believe that "time is valuable," so the idea of not using our time to accomplish something material feels wasteful. But time isn't valuable at all. In fact, time doesn't exist.**

It's just a system that people have created to measure the planet's rotation. Take the idea of "leap year," for example. Every four years, we add an extra day to the end of February. Why? Because the three years between every leap year are too short. So we add an extra day every four years to make up the math and stay on track with the earth's rotation. But get this, the Iranian calendar *doesn't* use mathematical rules to determine leap year, and the Chinese calendar adds an extra month every three years instead of an extra day.

Going even deeper into the illusion of time, we can look to the work of Italian theoretical physicist and author Carlo Rovelli. In his book *The Order of Time*, he profoundly points out that time is *elastic*. For instance, if you placed a precision timepiece at the top of a mountain and the same watch at sea level, the watch on the mountain would run faster. This happens because the gravitational waves of the earth slow down everything closest to its center. The same phenomenon is also responsible for this weird fact: if you were to travel into deep space, when you returned home, you would have aged a fraction of the time of everyone on your planet. I know it sounds like science fiction, but it's science fact.

What does considering all this wonky information about time tell us? That the stress we feel to pressure ourselves into action because time is running short is nothing more than a conditioned way of thinking. Because of this, open space or "reflection time" has lost its value to us on a fundamental level. This puts us in a bind.

We know that giving our nervous systems a break from any input is wise, yet we don't want to miss out on the chance to keep accomplishing. So we consider sitting on the couch with our phones or laptops a way to decompress. Nothing against doing that—it's fun—but it's not really decompression. Every video you watch, link you click, or post you make is causing your brain to problem-solve and exert computational energy. So even though you might be lying on the couch watching puppy videos all evening, your brain is still drained like it's playing a four-hour chess game.

> **Having constant input while engaging in endless tasks fries our nerves, pulls our attention away from the present, and puts it a few minutes into the future. This leaves us disconnected from our intuition, unable to hear the deeper parts of ourselves, and unclear about the direction in which we should be living our lives.**

Living like this burns us out and causes us to lose perspective of ourselves and the big picture too. The truth is that we can *manage* to exist in this way of being for our entire lives. However, just because we can get by like this doesn't mean it's our best option. At the very least, it will certainly not lead to a richer human experience.

How to Practice Stillness

We've established that time is an illusion and the only place we can exist is in the present. That means there is no reason to stress about *being* without *doing*. We only ever "are." Everything else we add to our existence in the present is a mental story. Now that we've got the upper hand on time, let's gain a deeper understanding of what stillness is and the various ways we can practice it.

What is stillness? It's the easiest thing you'll ever do. Because stillness is doing nothing. Being still is the act of consciously being present without engaging with your surroundings. If you wanted to practice stillness right now, all you'd have to do is put down this book, put your hands in your lap, and breathe.

> **Just exist.**
> **Stillness isn't about adding activities.**
> **It's about subtracting them.**

Overcoming Resistance

As we just covered, the actual act of stillness is simple. It's just sitting and doing nothing. Getting there can be hard. Because we're always fooling ourselves with the belief that we "don't have time," it's too easy to look at practicing stillness like something we need to bump from our to-do list because we're too busy. That's nonsense. Everyone can carve out 5 to 10 spare minutes a day. We only feel we can't because we're riding a wave of anxiety and tension and are too used to holding on to let go.

> **Like the Zen proverb goes, "If you don't have 10 minutes to meditate, then you need to meditate for two hours."**

Resistance is what we face when we go to be still. It's the mental barrier that arises right as we are about to take meaningful action. The feeling of resistance is like we're suddenly draped in lead weights and are physically incapable of doing what we desire. Of course, that feeling is all mental. It arises when we go to be creative, do something new, or work toward a goal. In short, resistance is our brain trying to conserve energy. The key to overcoming it is *recognizing* the feeling for what it is when it appears. As you're about to act, you will notice the feeling of resistance holding you back. All you have to do is note it, even say to yourself, "I feel resistance." Then immediately push through it without hesitation, almost like ripping a Band-Aid off with a single motion.

Here's how this could go down while you're attempting to practice stillness:

- You are in the middle of going from one task to the next.
- The thought enters your mind to stop and be still.
- Resistance stops you and gives you a reason to reconsider.
- You recognize the feeling for what it is.
- Ignore the feeling and start practicing stillness right away.

The key to overcoming resistance is taking immediate action in the face of the feeling. Resistance is a thin membrane. It feels like a steel door that's three feet thick. But it's truly so thin you can see the light through it. All you have to do is take one step forward, and you'll break through the feeling of resistance and be free to do whatever you desire. Breaking through resistance also gets easier every time you do it. The first time it will seem like a huge lift. The fifth time it will seem tough but doable. The tenth time it's an effortless motion.

Sit and Do Nothing

There are many ways you can practice stillness. Of course, the best one is the one that works for you and suits your lifestyle. We will start with a method that's informal, basic, and guaranteed to be achievable.

First, I'd suggest that you practice stillness at the same time every day. That may not be possible, depending on your schedule. But it's best to plug it into the same slot in your daily routine. Practicing stillness at the same time every day makes it a habit. Of course, that's good because it lowers the chances of you forgetting about it or seeing it as expendable.

Practicing stillness at any time of day is good. The morning is lovely because it clears your mind and relaxes your body first thing so you can take that energy into your day. Practicing in the evening is great, too, as it's an effective way to release the stress of the day, wind down, and get better sleep. Doing it during the middle of the day is also wonderful if you can swing it. Especially when you need a minibreak to reset your mindset amid a flurry of activity.

Make your practice simple. Remember what it's called: stillness. Not look-at-your-phone-ness. If you like, you can set a timer for 5, 10, or 20 minutes—however long you'd like to practice.

Getting Ready

- Turn off the music, laptop, and television.
- Make the space as quiet and calm as possible.
- Go outside if you have roommates or prefer nature.
- Sit on a couch, in a chair, on the ground, or in bed.
- Put your hands in your lap.
- Close your eyes.

Practicing

- Start taking calm breaths.
- Allow yourself to be still.
- Exist without any urgency.
- Open your senses.
- Listen to the sounds.
- Feel the present moment.
- Let yourself *be* without *doing*.
- Relax and sink deep into yourself.
- Breathe slow.
- Be.

As you practice being still, notice the feeling of your body decompressing. Feel the tension releasing from your muscles. Watch how your mind stops trying to calculate what's next and starts focusing on the richness of the present moment. Feel how you're reconnecting to your inner world. Notice how you are grounding yourself in the effervescent tapestry of existence.

Now that we've had some fun with stillness, let's have a quick look at meditation. Meditation is like stillness, but is an *active* practice, rather than a *passive* one. We are no longer just sitting there sinking into the present. In meditation, we are *actively* going on a discovery mission into Now.

Meditation

Meditation is undoubtedly one of the most transformative practices you can invite into your life. I will assume that I don't need to sing its praises here. Meditation has become so popular in our culture that there is an article, social post, book, or podcast talking about its life-changing power everywhere you look.

Here's something fun to consider that underlines how useful meditation is. What other activity can you think of that's *free* and available to all of us that gets so much attention and is so heavily promoted? Maybe exercise comes to mind. It's almost free, but you have to buy shoes, clothes, and perhaps a gym membership. Not meditation. It's actually free. You can do it anytime, anywhere, and no membership is required. It's always available to you, and you don't have to squeeze into activewear to get it done.

Almost everyone you ask if meditation is a good thing will say yes—even if they don't meditate. We all know it will make us calm, clear-minded, and compassionate.

So why do so many people struggle to *actually* practice it on a regular basis?

- **Reason 1:** They meditate until they feel the effects and then stop until they become stressed and need it again.

  Getting into this cycle is common. It's similar to how some people treat their diet. They eat well until they get to a level of fitness they're happy with, then slowly drift back to eating poorly until they decide to reel in the calories again. Treating meditation like this is self-defeating. It's great that a person recognizes they're stressed and starts meditating daily until they feel relief. But why stop when you start feeling good? It's like a person goes, "Ah, it's working! I think I'll quit." If you're doing something that makes you feel good, you should *keep doing it* to keep feeling good. Plus, meditation pays huge compound interest. The longer you do it consecutively, the more the benefits stack up.

- **Reason 2:** They want to meditate but forget to do so.

  Solving this problem comes down to understanding how to build habits effectively. As I mentioned earlier, the best way to build a new habit is to place it in the middle of a sequence of existing habits. If you wash your face and brush your teeth before bed, insert your meditation practice after brushing your teeth. That way, you're already in the habit of doing activities #1 (washing face) and #2 (brushing teeth), so #3 (meditating) will naturally tack on the end of the sequence. Also, #2 will *remind* you to do #3. Another useful way to remember to meditate is to make it visible. If you have a pillow or cushion you sit on to meditate, leave it in a spot where you'll be sure to see it. Doing this is leaving yourself a visual cue that will spark your memory and take you off autopilot.

- **Reason 3:** They are unsure if they are doing it right, so they get discouraged and stop.

  After teaching thousands of people how to meditate, I learned that *so many people* have meditation imposter syndrome. Trying to meditate is intimidating to people because it's an intentional mental activity. Because of that, there is no material feedback you can use to track your progress. For example, if you want to learn to run an eight-minute mile, it's clear what to do and whether you were successful. However, if you are trying to reduce your stress and clear your mind, it can be tricky to tell if you're doing it right. I have a lot of thoughts about this, but I'll keep it simple. *Meditation is easy.* It's so basic that anyone can do it. And that's what creates the tension. People are not used to things being so straight-ahead and simple. So they overcomplicate it, get in their own heads, and doubt themselves into quitting. Don't do that to yourself. Remember that meditation is *your* practice. There is no right way. Keep it simple. Lower your expectations. Do what works for you and forget about the rest.

Now that we've erased some reasons you can't meditate, let's get to some techniques you can try.

Set Your Mindset

The last thing you should do is overthink meditation, make it too complicated, or expect to be levitating in the next 10 minutes. It's a form of stillness too. As I mentioned earlier, the difference is that stillness is passive and meditation is active. That means that as you sit and do nothing, you'll consciously control your focus and breath. So, physically, you're still doing nothing and being still. But mentally, you're using a few tricks to take the depth of your stillness to a whole new level.

> **Don't go into meditation with any assumptions. Remember: self-transformation is self-discovery. Allow your mind to be open, curious, and patient.**

Receive whatever arises in your experience and know that meditation is a subtle and soothing experience, not one that's going to turn your world upside down.

Get Comfortable

All you need to meditate is a comfortable place to sit down. Don't worry about buying a meditation pillow and cushion unless you plan on getting into a formal practice. You can sit on your couch, in a chair, on the floor, or on your bed. Feel free to sit cross-legged or not. Whatever you prefer. You can even lie down on your bed if you like. Really, what we're looking for is a place to park your body where you feel supported enough to relax fully. That's it. There's no mystical position to get into, no altar to sit in front of, and no incense to light. All that stuff is just ritualization. If you do that and it works for you, great. Keep doing it. But you don't need all that stuff to meditate.

> **All you need is your mind.**

Practice 1: Rising, Falling, Sitting

Sit in a comfortable position. Rest your hands in your lap. Sit up straight but don't tense. Close your eyes. Point your mental focus to your chest. Pay attention to your breath going in and out. Feel your chest rise and fall. Continue that for as long as you desire.

That's it. Sitting with your body relaxed and eyes closed while paying attention to your chest and breath is all there is to it.

As you practice this, try to stop controlling the flow of your inhales and exhales. Let go and allow it to operate naturally while still watching it with your mind.

Mark the action if your focus wanders and you can't concentrate on your breath.

When you breathe in, think, "Rising."

When you breathe out, think, "Falling."

When you are between breaths, think, "Sitting."

So while practicing, you would continuously think:

"Rising . . . falling . . . sitting.

Rising . . . falling . . . sitting.

Rising . . . falling . . . sitting."

Practice 2: Becoming Lighter

In this practice, you will find a comfortable place to sit down again. Since this practice focuses on relaxation and letting go, some people prefer to lie down while doing it.

Again, you will close your eyes. This time, you should intentionally start taking long and deep breaths. Allow them to be smooth, slow, and natural. It's not a theatrical thing. You don't need to make the breaths intense and performative.

Let the air slowly pull in and gently push out. If you like, you can count to 8 while inhaling, then count to 10 while exhaling. Doing this will help you pace your breathing while focusing your mind.

As you continue breathing like this, start relaxing your muscles as much as possible while you exhale. Take another inhale, then relax your muscles even more.

Keep repeating this process. On each exhale, relax your body more and more deeply. Eventually, you'll notice the larger muscles in your body are relaxed. Then, you'll start to notice all types of interesting sensations. You'll feel the bottoms of your feet, the back of your head, your forearms and fingers, or maybe the core of your stomach relax.

Continue relaxing as you exhale, and then try letting go as much as possible. Allow yourself to feel completely free and open. Feel the heaviness falling away. Let yourself exist in the present moment. Let go more and more until you feel nothing but the lightness of a present, aware, and awakened self.

Practice 3: Walking Meditation

When we think about stillness, we often think the point is to make our body still. While this is true, it is more of a means to an end than anything else. The reason we aim to still the body is so that it will become stable and unagitated. By doing that, we can let go and release the physical tension we're holding. Releasing the tension in our body gives our mind a break because it no longer has to monitor our physical activity. Giving our mind a break allows *it* to relax, leading to a *stillness of mind.*

> **When our mind is still, we gain immense calm and mental clarity, which feeds back to the body, keeping it open, fluid, and free from grasping.**

For these reasons, most stillness practices focus on parking and calming the body. However, everyone is different, and some people simply don't enjoy sitting still for extended periods of time.

Walking meditation is an excellent alternative to formal sitting meditation. With deep roots in Buddhism, this practice develops mindfulness while activating the body rather than stabilizing it. While walking, you use the movement of your body to drop into a type of flow while being mindful of how your body engages with the earth, which creates a stillness of mind.

Go to your favorite place to walk. A quiet and peaceful place is good but isn't necessary. Remember, from the clearest perspective, all sensations that flow into your mind are just that—sensations. The difference between hearing birds chirping in the forest or the honks of cars in Manhattan exists only in *how we relate to the sounds.* Sounds we label as peaceful and sounds we label as disruptive are both just information going into our senses. It's our attachment to the idea that one is "bad" and the other is "good" that causes them to influence our emotions.

> **When you let go of how you think things should be and embrace them for how they are, you discover that all things are equally beautiful.**

As you begin walking, remember to walk calmly and peacefully. Once again, take deep, smooth, and slow breaths. Keep your eyes straight ahead or down at the ground before you. You don't want to swivel your head, as it will make your attention wander.

Now, as you walk, mindfully pay attention to each foot as it rises and each foot as it touches the ground. Feel, again and again, the sensation of the foot rising and the foot meeting the earth again. Walk gently and with intention. As the great master of Zen Buddhism, Thich Nhat Hanh, would say, "Walk as if you are kissing the earth with your feet."

As you continue walking, synchronize your long breaths with your footsteps. Remain mindfully connected to your footsteps. Open your awareness. Drop deeper into a state of flow. And feel your mind become still, resting on a foundation of continuous physical motion.

Stillness Is Realness

I've been meditating and practicing stillness for over 20 years. It has been the ultimate tool in every aspect of my life.

> **Mindset is everything. How we look at the world is how it appears. By intentionally making our minds more calm, clear, and aware, we can change our reality's texture. Every situation that once seemed overwhelming, hopeless, or to be conspiring against us is flipped inside out.**

Quiet is clarity. Increasing our self-awareness and sturdiness of mind allows us to calmly view the world through multiple perspectives. Doing this helps us see various dimensions of reality, which allows us to live closest to the truth of what is and far away from the drama of our minds. That's the beauty part of a daily stillness practice—especially meditation.

> **Meditation pauses the story in our mind long enough for us to remember that our mind is always telling us a story.**

When we are reminded of that, we can see ourselves and reality with an immense clarity that allows us to act with clearer intentions, deeply understand others, and become a force of peace that inspires all those around us.

Another beautiful benefit to stilling your mind is that it allows you to hear your own inner voice more clearly. You become disconnected from yourself when you're oversaturated with the noise of the day and constantly seeking the next task. Slowing down and practicing stillness allows you to clear away the static and hear your intuitive guiding voice. Connecting to yourself—what you're feeling deep inside—allows you to live from your heart in the present moment rather than simply reacting mindlessly based on the past.

Bring some form of stillness into your life. It doesn't have to be a sitting or walking practice. What works for you is great. But whatever you do, don't ignore it. Give yourself the time to clear your mind, reset, and connect to yourself. If you don't, you are shortchanging yourself. You need time to reflect, let go, and integrate your daily experience. Without it, you'll continue to hold the static of your day and always wonder why your mind isn't as clear as you want it to be. With it, you'll feel light and clear and carry a perspective with you through life that is constantly in tune with the true nature of reality.

CHAPTER 16

TENSION IS TEMPORARY

I've spent a lot of time thinking deeply about the sources of our daily suffering. How is it that we are forced to feel a constant slow boil of dissatisfaction and stress by merely existing? It doesn't matter how healthy our lifestyle is, how kind we are, or if we dedicate all our time to altruistic pursuits. Those things help, but we'll still live with at least a small amount of suffering, tension, and unease. Some argue that it's possible to completely alleviate our suffering and transcend our animal nature. That's a nice idea. But I don't believe it. Like Ram Dass famously said, "If you think you're enlightened go spend a week with your family." But seriously, I think the idea of living completely free of suffering is an idealized notion that's meant to inspire us to exceed what we thought was possible for ourselves. As in, if we want to get to the top of the mountain, we shouldn't aim for the top. If we do, we'll probably hit the middle. If we want to hit the top of the mountain, we should aim for the sky.

A *part* of being human is being stuck in the middle of joy and disappointment, pleasure and pain, and stress and relaxation. These qualities are a part of who we are on a root level. Because we're emotional beings with big egos, we're always looking for our preferences to be pandered to. We want a little more satisfaction, a little more attention, a bit more materialism, and even . . . a little more enlightenment. That's why humans are great explorers but not so great at letting things rest as they are. The cosmic joke of the matter is that we all feel entitled to *more* and having *our way,* when there is no *way* to be had. We are small blips in a giant self-organizing whirlpool of existential chaos.

In other words, we all suffer because we hold on to our mental tension.

> **We are *designed* to want to control the flow of nature and feel like we're better than the next person. But it's all a fool's errand because nature doesn't care about any of that. It's all in our heads. The trees, ocean, and sky don't care about the smoothness of our skin, the thickness of our bank accounts, or the number of our social followers. They just are.**

Yet we get epically wrapped up in the story of our identities while trying to play the human game. Then we suffer because we can't let go and exist purely in the present outside of the trappings of our ego.

Understanding the Problem

Don't worry. Laying all this out isn't meant to make you feel hopeless or like you will be stuck suffering through tension forever. We're just diagnosing the problem. Which is that as long as we're alive, we *will* experience tension—but because moments of tension are often unexpected, we forget they're temporary.

This misunderstanding causes many of our problems. When our day is going fine and we're hit with a wave of tension, we feel like it will last forever. Thankfully, moments of peak suffering are few and far between. That's not to say that if you have a stressful life, you don't feel them several times a day. By "few and far between" I mean that they come in short bursts rather than marathons. When we feel swells of suffering, they burn extra hot because we aren't used to their intensity.

When we experience suffering, we make decisions *in reaction to our feelings of tension.* We do this because as we're experiencing the feeling of tension in the moment, it feels like that's all there is or ever will be. That's the ironic thing about moments of suffering. They have the power to bring us closer to the present than almost anything else. That's because when we're full of tension, our whole body lights up, our mindset shifts, and we are *actively* uncomfortable. All the noise in our minds that normally distracts us becomes less important.

When this happens, we become highly focused on our pain and how we might resolve it. Because suffering brings us to the cutting edge of the present moment, we become aware of many things we might not have noticed before. Unfortunately, because tension is a form of energy, we look for ways to displace that negative energy to burn off our suffering.

In other words, when we feel a blast of anxiety, fear, sadness, anger, or frustration, we tend to express it toward ourselves, others, or our situation. We do this because we feel overwhelmed with negative energy and are looking for a way to get it out. Because our awareness is sharpened when we're suffering, our mind becomes more present. This experience is jarring to someone not used to being present because being in the present feels infinite. So when someone is brought to the present by their suffering, it gives them the illusion that they will feel that passing pain forever.

Dealing with Tension

When we are in a whirlwind of suffering, we may feel like it will never end. But it always does. Think about how much of your life is spent feeling relatively middle of the road. That's what the majority of life is. Long stretches of rather bland day-to-day activity that don't have a ton of resonance one way or the other.

Because these long stretches of normalness are pretty forgettable, we easily forget them. No one remembers when they sat on their couch four months ago, rewatching their favorite TV series all night, with everything feeling right in the world.

However, moments of tension are peak experiences. So that makes them much easier to remember. Not because they are special in any way but because they are novel. Even then, the experiences that stick out because they are less ordinary are *still* forgotten. Think back to when you were flustered in a wave of mental tension three times ago. You can't remember it. You *might* remember the most recent time you felt that way. But even a few times before that has evaporated into the ether of infinity. Hilarious, isn't it?

> **We take our moments of tension so seriously when they arise. We allow ourselves to make bad decisions and believe that the weight of the world is on us. When really, those waves of tension are simple, momentary, often meaningless, and always forgettable little windows of time.**

The Power of Impermanence

A central idea in Buddhism is that all things that come into existence will also go out of existence. Another way to say it is that everything changes, and nothing lasts forever. This concept is called *impermanence*. Initially, this concept can feel somewhat dark to people, leaving them thinking, "What? Everything dies forever and always until the end of time—even time itself? Thanks, I hate it."

People have that reaction because the notion of impermanence directly pricks their attachments, creating reactionary feelings of grasping about life, death, and everything that they hold close.

But if we can let go of those attachments a little, we can see that impermanence is a beautiful way to describe the flow of existence.

There are several large trees in my yard. While thinking, I like to look out the window and stare at them. As the back part of my mind is calculating whatever I'm trying to work out, the front part of my mind is in awe at the living poetry of the tree. It so perfectly exhibits the flow of life. The trees are at least a few decades old, so they have a sense of being about them. They sprout lush leaves that flourish, which, after a few months, fall off and are absorbed into the soil. The tree lives bare branched for several months. Then new leaves sprout again.

I've watched this happen year after year to these trees. The leaves exist. Then they don't. Then they do. Even though the leaves look the same each year, they aren't the same leaves from the previous year. They are new. But that's not the point. The point is that they are *life* that continues to emerge, vanish, and emerge.

Looking around at every other aspect of existence, we can see it all is impermanent. Every animal, plant, person, and even *planet* is undergoing a process of change, like the trees in my yard. The only difference is the timetable that they are on. Now, when people think about impermanence, their attachments cause them to focus on the decaying aspect of things. It's hard not to. Most of us only become aware of the importance of something *after* we bond with it. Seeing a beautiful flower growing in our yard isn't instantly meaningful. We have to notice it several times, see it after it's bloomed, then start to count on seeing it again. Only then does the bloomed flower have meaning to us. That's because it holds a place in our lives. We hope seeing it will give us a dose of beauty that will lift our spirits. So we become attached to things that already have a presence. Because of that, we get used to only thinking about what is meaningful to us as fading away.

I used to think about impermanence like this too. It seemed like a hyperrealistic way of viewing the world. One that wasn't romantic but was effective at teaching us that we should be present with what's important to us while it's here, because it will eventually pass. Then one day it struck me that I was only thinking about half of the equation.

> **If impermanence means that all things are constantly going out of existence, there must be an equal number of things constantly *coming into* existence.**

Otherwise, we'd run out of stuff altogether. This insight struck me, and I began to refer to it as "the upside of impermanence." After sitting with the idea for a while, I began to consider how we fit into the coming and going of existence. Interestingly, our human experience is caught right in the middle. We are constantly coming into existence and going out of existence at the same time.

Letting Go

What does it mean to be coming and going at the same time? It means we unavoidably exist in the present moment—even if our minds are elsewhere. We are constantly changing and growing while leaving behind old parts of ourselves that are no longer who we want to be. That means that just like the trees in my yard, we lose some leaves each season, spend a little time recovering, then bloom fresh, new leaves when we're ready.

It can be difficult to see this change as it happens because it occurs so gradually over time. But it's easy to see if we zoom out and reflect on our lives. If you think about what was important to you, how you dressed, what your interests were, and how you acted 10 years ago, you'd likely be unrecognizable in contrast to who you are today. That's because, throughout that time, you have been in a constant flow with impermanence. You've left behind what wasn't for you anymore and grown into new things that are.

See, you're a natural. You've been embracing the power of impermanence all along without realizing it. And when you think about it this way, impermanence loses the negative vibe that some people initially feel about it. Considering the upside of impermanence shows us that always being able to change and let things pass through us is not only responsible for our personal evolution but a necessary feature of being human.

Tension Is Temporary

Now that we've thought about how useful impermanence is and how good we are at it, we should put it into action. I mean, think about it: if you're already this good at leaving behind stuff so you can grow, imagine how good you'd be if you were doing it *intentionally.*

Let's return to the beginning of this chapter, where we discussed how mental tension troubles our lives. When most people feel tension, they're overwhelmed by the emotions and intensity of it. So they usually react in whichever way they are conditioned. Often this looks like avoidance. People will try to ignore their tension and create an inner emotional wall until the storm passes. Others try to numb themselves with substances or distractions. Sometimes, people will take their tension out on others. They feel the wave of negativity inside them and look to whoever is nearby to lay their tension on, hoping that it will drain from them. Of course, this isn't a good method. It doesn't relieve the person who initially felt the suffering and spreads the pain like a sickness to an innocent bystander.

None of these approaches to dealing with tension are healthy. And they certainly don't resolve anything. So if it's true that we'll always have to deal with tension, stress, and suffering, then what's the best thing for us to do? Confront it head-on. As you continue to do the work and become self-aware, you can have a greater sense of what arises inside you. I'm sure you've had some experience with this. At one point in your life, you would be somewhat shocked by tension when it appeared, almost as if lightning struck you. But now, after being on the path a little while, you probably notice the *swell* of tension as it enters your body instead of it coming as a complete shock.

Being able to notice when you start to feel inner tension rising is an incredible skill that opens many opportunities for growth. Cultivating mental space allows you to mindfully deal with your tension.

> **Controlling how you react to the initial feelings of suffering makes it possible for you to put distance between your feelings and your actions. Instead of reacting and being taken over by the intensity of frustration, you can see it coming and start letting go *as the tension is rising.***

Doing this is a powerful move, as it prevents you from becoming attached to your suffering and getting swept up in a mindset of mindless anger or anxiousness.

Mindfully noticing when you feel a burst of tension coming on allows you to face the intensity of what you're feeling head-on, then let it go. Think about this as if you're turning yourself into a window through which your temporary suffering can simply pass.

For example, an unaware person would be caught off guard by their tension, hold it inside of them, and then sit with it until it diffuses on its own. This can take hours or even days. And considering how much suffering shifts our mindsets to a negative place, this is not the outcome we want. It will increase our potential to express negativity toward ourselves and others. On the other hand, if you're self-aware, you will notice when the earliest feelings of tension are rising. You can then use your mindful strength to pause, recognize the tension for what it is so you don't become attached to it, then consciously let it go.

The first few times you practice doing this, it's likely that it won't go as smoothly as you envision. That's okay and to be expected. Like any practice, it takes time to familiarize yourself with the process and feel your way through it. Once you have some experience, it becomes easier and more natural. Eventually, noticing your tension and letting it pass through you becomes second nature—as basic as exhaling a breath.

While developing this skill of releasing your tension, it's useful to remember the power of impermanence. This, among other reasons, is why I raised the concept and walked us through what it means and how it looks in life.

> **Knowing that *everything* in life—no matter how permanent it feels—is in a constant state of transition is extremely liberating. When we feel the shock of suffering, we can instantly remember that even though this feels huge, it's nothing more than another passing sensation that will be forgotten like all the rest.**

Keeping this perspective close helps create the space needed to prevent us from becoming attached to our mental tension when it appears.

Once you embody the truth of impermanence, you can effortlessly turn yourself into a window when suffering comes. You can see it coming, note it, and let it go all in a single motion. Sure, there may be no way to completely escape feeling tension in our lives. But if we face it head-on and actively work with it when it arises, we can allow it to merely pass us by rather than inviting it inside to live with us.

Let's take a look at how letting go plays out in real life:

1. **You notice tension rising in your body or mind.**

   Typically, you'll feel your heart rate rise, your muscles tense, and your breathing quicken. You'll also likely start to feel hot because your adrenal glands release stress hormones when you're flustered. Your mind will start racing, you'll become hyperaware, and you'll have trouble focusing.

2. **You'll feel the impulse to react.**

   After automatic responses take over your body, you'll feel a strong urge to do anything to respond to the intensity that you're feeling. This is where mindful awareness is valuable. Having a spaciousness of mind allows you to notice your impulses but hold back from reacting so that you're able to proceed intentionally.

3. **You choose to release your tension and reset.**

   Next, you'll take several deep breaths and reset your body. What you're doing here is *undoing* the physical tension that manifests after your body releases stress hormones. You'll want to consciously relax your muscles, calm your breathing, and ground yourself. Doing this gives you greater mental clarity, which helps you shift your perspective, see the tension as a passing phenomenon, release it, reset it, and move forward with self-compassion.

> **Perspective is power. Remembering that tension is temporary and you have the *choice* to shift your mindset gives you the strength to control not how you feel, but who you are.**

Don't Let Letting Go Turn into Resentment

Learning to let inner tension flow by without grasping it is a powerful skill that will add many benefits to your life. It will keep you from getting wrapped up in meaningless stress, burning yourself out with anger, and creating conflicts where there don't need to be. However, being clear about *why* you are letting your tension pass is important. The goal of developing this skill is to minimize the time you spend suffering and to keep you from being reactive when you're overwhelmed by frustration.

The goal is *not* to use this skill to practice avoidance. People often do this in relationships as an innocent attempt to keep tensions low during conflicts. However, if they do this without *communicating* with their partner, it can easily turn into avoidance, which then grows into resentment.

Here's how this can play out. Say a person is working to consciously let go of their tension in a relationship. They always do their best to increase their mindful strength, but their partner does not. In conflicts or even day-to-day issues, the thoughtful person is great at being peaceful, not holding tension toward their partner, and keeping the big picture in mind. So they're able to resist holding tension. Yet they start to resent the fact that *they* always have to be the ones doing the work.

While this might seem like the person practicing mindfulness in this situation is keeping the peace, they are mistaking passiveness for peacefulness. They've taken a good first step in learning to let their tension pass through them without attachment. However, they have yet to learn that just because you don't *hold* your tension doesn't mean that further action isn't required.

For example, if your partner repeats a behavior that is frustrating to you, letting go of your reactive tension is a smart first step. The next step is calmly *communicating* the issue, how it makes you feel, and what your needs are. Doing this ensures you're mindfully working with your tension, while letting your partner know there is an issue to resolve. Active communication is how you keep the seeds of resentment from being planted.

Practicing this won't always be perfect. Don't expect it to be. We're all human, which means that none of us will get it right 100 percent of the time. But by putting forward the *effort* to let go of tension and thoughtfully communicate, you'll strengthen your connection to the people in your life—and yourself.

PART V

AN APPETITE FOR POSSIBLE THINGS

CHAPTER 17

REDEFINE YOURSELF OFTEN

People get used to the idea of who they are. They accept their self-perceived abilities, interests, and what they *think* they can do to make themselves feel more alive. Accepting who you are right now for all that you ever will be does a great disservice to your future self. I'm sure you know this and agree. And if you were asked if you do this, you'd likely say no. Yet, if we look at our habits, we'll often see that we limit ourselves without realizing it.

We like to *feel* like we're allowing ourselves to be open, grow, and move toward a higher version of who we are. But in reality, we're usually pretty stagnant. That's because, above anything else, we like to feel comfortable. Life is complicated and exhausting. It's hard to turn down the things that give us a sense of familiar safety. While there's certainly a time and place for comfort, there also has to be balance.

> **If we're ever going to feel *alive*, like the wind is blowing at our backs, and we're on the exciting edge of breaking through into another, greater layer of our own existence, we have to *seek out the new.***

Before we go further, let's consider what it means to redefine who we are. It's important to understand that doing this doesn't have to be dramatic. Nor should it be. We aren't talking about waking up one day, buying all new clothes, quitting our job, and becoming a traveling street musician. Making major changes quickly isn't always bad, but it *is* always impulsive. Acting impulsively is a form of *reacting,* which means that it's a conditioned response. Reacting in this way is usually a form of avoidance. Doing this distracts us with change or chaos rather than dealing with the real issue. Remember, balance is key to making smart and authentic moves forward.

When we talk about redefining ourselves, we are talking about smaller, more nuanced changes that add up to larger changes over time. For example:

- We might notice ourselves entertaining negative self-talk before we do something important. In that moment, we can stop, recognize the story we're telling ourselves, and think, "No. That's not who I am anymore. I've grown. I'm capable. And I won't be a person who talks down to myself anymore."
- We could be someone who doesn't like to hang out with large groups of people. The next time we get an invitation to go out with a group, we could feel resistance. Then we might consider that we're operating off an old narrative about ourselves, and truthfully, we don't know that we wouldn't enjoy it. So we stop thinking, "I'm a person who doesn't like large groups," and explore ourselves by trying it out again with an open mind.
- We could be attached to the idea that we have to dress or wear our hair a certain way. Being stuck on our appearance can make us feel trapped in the past and unable to express who we are. Embracing the fact that you can look however you want while letting go of your old forms of thinking is a way to redefine who you are and become more free.

- We could also look at what we do for a living as all that's possible. Then we could redefine ourselves by realizing that we are allowed to explore, find out who we are *today*, and move toward a new kind of profession that we thought we weren't "allowed" to do because of how we had previously defined ourselves.

These are a few examples of ways to redefine ourselves in life. Of course, there are countless areas in which we can evolve who we *think we have to be* into who we feel we are in the present moment. Anything can be redefined, like what foods we eat, what music we listen to, what kinds of people we spend time with, what books we read, and what movies we watch. Or big things like our relationships, spiritual practices, or where we live.

> **The reason redefining ourselves is important is because it gives us *freedom*. Staying stuck in old ways of thinking means we're leaning in to conditioned behavior. Those behaviors are the parts of our lives that are on autopilot. And if we're always on autopilot, it means that we are not *thinking for ourselves*.**

If we aren't thinking for ourselves, it means that we are allowing who we are to be *defined* by the patterns of the past. However, if we are present and *actively* choose to explore who we are, we can take charge of our lives, keep growing, and continue to breathe in the exciting energy of what it means to be alive.

The Greats Are Great for a Reason

Redefining ourselves is all about learning to be open. We have to be open to new ideas, experiences, and paths in our lives. To reject the invitation of the new is to become numb to life itself.

There's no better place to see an example of how a single person can evolve than by looking at the life of an artist. Artists are clear examples because the good ones are always looking to elevate their work. They stay open as much as they can and try to perceive the world as if it's for the first time so that they can see reality clearly, without the blockage of their own judgment. Living in the flow of change allows artists to evolve their work—and themselves—at an inspiring pace. This is why when you look back at the lives of the greats, it appears that they figured out how to live many lives within the span of one.

Take legendary jazz musician Miles Davis, for example. He started out playing bebop in the 1940s. He helped lay the foundation for the sounds of what most people hear in their heads when they hear the word *jazz*. You know, the smooth, calm, swinging coffee-shop vibe that's almost a cliché. Six phases later, Miles could be found in the early 1970s with his trumpet plugged into a wah-wah pedal, running into a Marshall guitar amp, wearing crazy giant sunglasses, playing electrified funk with classical Indian instruments added to the mix like a worldly jazz Jimi Hendrix.

We could also look at the life of one of the greatest, if not *the* greatest, comedians of all time—George Carlin. George started off doing basic, squeaky-clean comedy with a partner in the 1960s. By the time the 1990s rolled around, he'd gone solo, been through a handful of identities, come up with the "seven dirty words," and started wearing all black and raging against society and most people in it. Going from being a clean-shaven, suit-wearing guy impersonating a game show host to saying, "It's called the American Dream, because you have to be asleep to believe it" is quite an identity transformation.

What's wild is that we can even look at artistic evolutions that are still happening before our eyes. Check out Taylor Swift. She's one of the biggest stars on the entire planet, has sold over 100 million records, and has won a dozen Grammys at the time I'm writing this (and likely more by the time you're reading it). It's easy to forget that even though she has been crushing the pop music world for over a decade, she started as a country singer-songwriter.

Somehow, a teenage country artist bloomed into a pop superstar who has earned over half a billion dollars.

How is it that these three artists and countless others have been able to grow in such legendary ways that they defined what it meant to be a legend along the way? It's because they are present and always open to what's next. None of these artists cling to the idea that they have to live inside a box, fearing what other parts of themselves they might find if they start paying attention. They actively, passionately, and artfully pay attention to what they *feel*, allow themselves to stay open, question who they are, and continue moving into a version of themselves that is more greatly realized.

Now, we shouldn't expect ourselves to transform with the force of Taylor, George, or Miles. Taking a quick look at those artists' careers was meant to highlight the mechanism of change and what's possible at the highest level. The lives of those artists are reminders that, in our own way, we can stay open, keep redefining who we are, and continue evolving on our own journeys. Huge changes aren't always good or necessary either.

> **It's not about how much you change. It's about how well you listen to your inner compass and let yourself grow when needed.**

Watching for Portals

Say you've decided that you're going to be proactive and open and redefine yourself more often. Deciding that is a great first step. The second step is learning how to actually do it. As always, your awareness is your superpower. Now that self-evolution is at the forefront of your mind, you'll start to notice patterns of thinking, being, and doing that feel stale or resistant. Being mindful of when those feelings arise is important. These signals that go off inside you always try to communicate a deeper truth. Not necessarily a universal truth, but a truth that is meaningful to you. *Your truth.* The insights you need to have to become a happier, more enlightened, and empowered version of yourself.

The 13th-century poet Rumi is supposed to have once said, "What you seek is seeking you." And he wasn't joking. Listening to our inner signals is how we're able to tell *what* it is about ourselves that we would do well to redefine. I like to call these feelings *portals*.

> **When the timing is right, we become self-aware, a few things outside of us happen to line up, and we get magical invitations to become a higher version of who we are.**

I think of these moments as openings in time, where we can pass from one dimension to the next, like a multiverse. For those who are unfamiliar, multiverse theory suggests we live in one potential timeline of reality that has its own version of how things are. Next to it are infinite alternate universes where reality is just a little different. When these portals of opportunity open, I imagine they are like windows into slightly different universes. If we desire, we can walk through them and shift reality ever so slightly. To be clear, I don't literally think that's what's happening. But it's a fun way to think about it. And if you think about it long enough, it makes sense. You know, your reality and everything you know is one way. Then you choose to change your behavior and reality changes around you. So, in a strange way, changing ourselves is like changing to an alternate universe where a different version of you exists.

We want to learn how to identify these portals and decide whether to walk through them and change our reality or not. However, there are a couple of different kinds of portals that we should be aware of. There are internal portals and external ones. Some invite us to change how we think. Others invite us to alter our path or make personal strategic changes. All of them have a fun feeling of magic if you're open and playful enough. And that's an essential element to this and all aspects of self-growth and change.

Sure, we want to grow, become more self-aware, and raise up our lives, but that doesn't mean we shouldn't take it lightly and have fun while doing it. If anything, the joy you bring to your path will wind through the fabric of your journey, infusing your wisdom with a sense of playfulness and curiosity. This will give you more longevity and dilate your ability to perceive and navigate the true nature of reality.

The Inner Landscape

Before we move on to talking about the different types of portals, let's understand how to spot them in the first place. Being more mindful of your thoughts, feelings, and actions will raise your awareness of your inner landscape. By inner landscape, I mean the spacious playing field of activity that's going on inside of you at any given moment. Let's visualize this so you can see your inner landscape more clearly.

Consider that there is a spacious presence in your mind and body at every moment. In this space, you feel the physical sensations of emotions, like the fire of anger or the swelling warmth of love. You can also feel your intuition in this space. When you're in the middle of making a decision, you can feel a magnetic pull in your stomach and heart area. Also, when you're putting energy into your intellect when trying to think of something, you'll feel churning in your mind.

These feelings in our inner landscape are fascinating and insightful once you become aware of them. As you turn your attention inward and start being more mindful of these sensations, you might first notice a lot of noise. That's natural. Think of your inner landscape as a garden. For your whole life, it's gone untended, and the plants and weeds have grown wild. Now, you're looking at these mental formations for the first time and seeing them overgrown. Don't let the messiness turn you off. Simply start paying attention to your inner world of thoughts and feelings, and like a garden, you'll start to get rid of the weeds by addressing what is arising in you.

A beautiful thing happens after you pay attention to your inner landscape for a while. Once you've spent time with it and it's well tended, it will take on a clear and peaceful state of being. With that peacefulness comes immense mental clarity. If we remember from earlier, mental clarity doesn't mean that we have a mind with no thoughts. It means that we've tended to our minds enough to be aware of our thoughts as they arise. As we start experiencing this, our internal landscape becomes broad, open, and crystal clear. This spaciousness makes it incredibly easy to identify what arises in us at any given moment.

For example, in the past, we might have had an impulse to say something cutting during a frustrating conversation. Typically, we would reactively say the mean remark without real awareness of our actions. Only after we spoke the words in the heat of the moment would we become aware of what we said, the kind of energy it carried, or how harmful it was to the other person. With inner spaciousness, we would notice the *impulse* or desire to say a mean remark as it forms in our mind. That clarity allows us to think with a larger and more compassionate perspective and let go of the impulse to express a harmful comment before saying it.

> **Building a strong, mindful connection to our inner landscape gives us the power to understand what's happening inside of us. This skill helps us shape who we are and connect more intimately with the inner workings of our thoughts and feelings.**

By being more connected to ourselves, we become more aware of the nuances inside us. These nuances take shape in the form of resistance, avoidance, conditioned behaviors, and mindless behavior patterns. Learning to notice these things *as they rise* is how we can identify *what we want to redefine about ourselves.*

When our inner landscape is clear, we can notice a combination of emotion, dissonance, and a higher awareness that questions our actions. All these things hitting at once is like an alarm going off inside of us, telling us that we aren't in alignment with our current state of action. It's then that we question why we're acting a certain way and evolve our identities by choosing to take *different* actions in real time. Each time we redefine ourselves in this way, we release an old story of who we have to be and liberate our current self, freeing us from the conditioned patterns of the past and allowing us to fully thrive in the present.

Passing through Portals

We're going to use the great Miles Davis as our example to understand what these portals of personal change look like. He's a great example, not only because he went through so much change in his life but because he innovated for decades. And he did it all in the face of massive cultural resistance. Because of this, he took on a key quality in developing strong and constant personal change—he stopped caring what other people thought.

Now, that isn't to say that we should close ourselves off from feedback and the insights of others—quite the opposite. Humbly listening to trusted friends is not only valuable, it's crucial. The people closest to us have a view of us that we can't have. They can see us from the outside, see our blind spots, and understand a different *context* of how we are moving through life. Listening to those trying to help us is the only way we can shine a light on our blind spots and become well-rounded, flourishing humans.

On the other hand, we shouldn't get hung up on what we *think* others are thinking about us. That can keep us stuck in the story of who we are because we believe we have to play a role that we imagine other people are comfortable with. One of the powerful moves Miles made was that he stopped caring what *he* thought *other people* thought about him and his music and just started living based on what *felt right* and true for him. But we're getting ahead of ourselves in understanding the story of Miles. So let's start a little earlier in his journey.

As we touched on at the top of this chapter, Miles Davis was one of the musicians who helped build the foundation of modern jazz music. While attending the Juilliard School of Music in the 1940s, he became increasingly fascinated with saxophonist Charlie Parker, who was instrumental in developing bebop jazz. Miles went to the clubs and tried to get onstage and play as much as possible. After a few semesters, he dropped out of Juilliard.

- **Portal:** Dropping out of school so that he could play music full time in the clubs was one of the early portals Miles walked through. Consider what was happening in his internal landscape during that time. He was burning inside with a passion for playing music and was only in school to make his father happy and have a reason to live in New York City. After he spent time in the clubs rubbing elbows with some of his biggest musical inspirations, he felt something. What arose on his internal landscape and irresistibly pulled at his intuition was that he didn't need to finish school. What was the point? The only reason he was going was to figure out how to play music full time.

  He saw the portal that opened that would allow him to do that if he walked through it. So he let go of the story that he was a kid going to music school. He then redefined himself as a professional musician who didn't care what his father or teachers at Juilliard thought. Miles decided to write a new story that he was the meanest trumpet player in town and would show his musical idols why *they* would want to play with *him*. And he did. Less than a year after he hit the clubs hard, he replaced the legendary Dizzy Gillespie in Charlie Parker's band.

After walking through that portal, Miles was cooking and had leveled up his situation. But that was only the start. He kept grinding, playing, and finding his way over the next decade, spending all his time writing music, playing with different legends, and overcoming his dependence on drugs and alcohol. During that time, he started to feel frustrated with how jazz was being played. Now, that's an easy thought to read about in a history book. But imagine *having* that thought in the moment: deciding that a whole genre of music—which was still young at the time—was somehow lacking. Miles knew that something had to change. And he was the one who was going to make it happen.

- **Portal:** As Miles spent every night playing in the clubs in New York, with the masters that had inspired him no less, he started to see, or should I say *hear*, the *matrix*. Being immersed in the musical language of the present helped him start to hear what was working about jazz and what was becoming stale and holding it back. So what was arising on his internal landscape was that a major innovation needed to happen. He experimented, studying some avant-garde approaches of the day, and decided to boldly redefine the theory of how jazz was being played. I'll save us from going through music theory school and make it quick. Up until that point, conventional jazz was played using a framework of chords. Miles decided to make his music modal. In short, that means that for his solos, he started using more simple chords. However, their starting notes had the freedom to move around on the base chord notes, creating deep, colorful, and moody music. By listening to what was arising in his inner landscape and walking through the portal he felt open, Miles invented the sound that made people say jazz sounds "cool." He redefined the story of what music should sound like, then used that approach to write a record called *Kind of Blue*, which changed music history forever, sold five

> million copies, and was declared a national treasure by the U.S. House of Representatives. Not bad for a Juilliard dropout.

Of course, someone like Mr. Davis has an extraordinarily rich story full of detail, struggle, and glory. I've just picked a few key moments in the legend's life to highlight for our purposes. When we consider this story of how Davis was looking inward, we can see that he was able to be so innovative because he refused to do anything other than *listen to his instincts*. He was in touch with his inner landscape, and when he became aware of something that *felt right,* he didn't let anything get in his way. He followed through until it became a reality. In the process, he was never attached to the story of who he was supposed to be. Early on, he defined himself as a verb instead of a noun. He knew he was not a predetermined thing. He was a being in a state of motion.

This process of self-transformation is helpful to remember while we are on our own journeys. Paying attention to your inner landscape and what feels right is how you can guide yourself into an ever-expanding future of potential. Of course, the key is to be present, watch and respect the portals that open inside you, and walk through them when it feels right.

Remember not to allow yourself to be defined. You can constantly let go of the story of who you think you have to be to keep growing into who you really are.

Like our friend Miles Davis, you, too, are a verb. The key to constant personal evolution is remembering that when you start feeling like a noun.

External Portals

So far, we've talked about paying attention to our internal landscape, being mindful when feelings and intuitions align, and taking action to redefine how we think of ourselves when the time is right. However, we shouldn't only focus on what's emerging and connecting inside of us. These intuitive invitations, or *portals*, exist outside of us too. We should watch for events, opportunities, and new pathways that arise in our lives and not let the cosmic winks of the universe pass us by.

It's strange, but every one of my major professional boosts has come from recognizing an external portal and being open and aware enough to walk through it. I'll take you through a few examples of how this has played out in my life so that you will have an easier time noticing these external portals in yours. Keep in mind, there have been dozens of these occurrences in my life, and I'd love to write about them all, but for now, I'll pick a few choice ones.

Even though I've been studying Eastern wisdom traditions, Western philosophy, psychology, and human consciousness since I was a teenager, early on, I never intended to make it a part of my professional life. While fervently exploring my mind, I was also equally obsessed with music. I composed music constantly, planning on making my way in the music industry as a composer. However, my musical tastes proved to be a problem. I like exotic sounds. And unless you're lucky, that's not a great quality if you want to sell enough music to make a living. Nevertheless, in my early 20s, I refused to give up and relentlessly wrote music, hoping I could find a way to make a living out of it. While I wasn't having a lot of success selling my music, something else interesting started happening.

Since I was trying to get myself out there as a composer, I knew a lot of other artists. I don't know if many of them liked my music, but I was sure they liked how it was produced. Friends would comment that my music sounded clear, deep, and three-dimensional and told me they had no idea how I achieved that. Eventually, some fellow artists asked me if I would do to their music whatever I had done to mine. I loved producing music, so I was happy to give them a hand and help produce their sounds. After a while, friends of friends would hear the work I'd done and reach out to me, asking if I would help them out for a hundred bucks. At the time, that seemed like an incredible payment to do something I loved. As word of mouth spread, more and more artists started reaching out to me, asking if they could pay me for my production skill. Then, I noticed an external portal had opened.

- **Portal:** Even though I had spent years thinking I would be a rock star-composer-artist type guy, I had truthfully noticed that it wasn't panning out. Right around the time I started to come to terms with the cold, hard fact that I wasn't making any financial progress as a composer, people began asking if they could pay me as a producer. I recognized this and realized that a portal had opened. This was an opportunity to still be involved in music but in a way that had never occurred to me until then. So I intentionally let go of the story that I had in my mind that I was going to make a living as a composer and redefined myself as someone who would make it as a producer. After focusing on it for a few short years, I found myself running my own professional audio mastering studio full time.

All through the time I was working as a professional mastering engineer, I was still deeply immersed in studying my inner life. When I was with my friends, if we weren't talking about music, we were talking about consciousness exploration, the strangeness of the universe, and how we could tap into some kind of cosmic energy to improve our lives. I was, and still am, incredibly passionate about the philosophy of mind and loved talking about it with anyone willing to go there with me. And even sometimes when people weren't.

Through a totally random chance, I caught wind of someone in my hometown of Austin asking for help setting up their podcast gear. They were also a consciousness explorer. Remember, this was in 2012, way before most people even knew what a podcast was. Podcasts were being recorded at kitchen tables, not million-dollar studios. So being a professional audio engineer and lifelong student of the mind, I was down to help this stranger get set up so they could start broadcasting meaningful conversations into the world. Turns out that we hit it off, and their podcast developed a sizable audience rather quickly. In no time, their audience members start e-mailing me, urging me to start up my own podcast.

- **Portal:** For years, I'd worked to build up my reputation as a composer, but I saw a portal open and redefined my path into a career as a producer. Now, even though things were going well in my music career, another, deeper part of who I was as a person was being called forward by the universe. I love music. But studying and exploring our inner lives hits way harder than that for me. That's why I'd never tried to do anything publicly or professionally with it. It was so important to me that I kept it safe by keeping it private.

  However, after guesting on a few podcasts, I got comfortable talking publicly about my inner life pursuits and was considering starting a podcast for fun. I mean, all I ever did was talk about this stuff with my friends, so why not share those conversations with others? Right at the time I was trying to decide if I wanted to start a podcast, people started asking me to take my studies and ideas public. I saw what was happening. I noticed how my music career was only a means to lead me to this bigger and more *true* path that the universe offered me. So in 2015 I decided to start a podcast. And shortly after that, I found myself doing it full time and being interviewed about it by *The New York Times*.

Finding Your Own Portals

What are we supposed to make of these strange moments in life where everything lines up just right? How can they be accidental when they seem to draw deeper things out of us that we didn't even know were possible, yet turn out to be exactly what we feel we are meant to be doing?

One school of thought on these occurrences is that they are divinely orchestrated. As if a universal fate or math equation is unraveling for us all, and we are simply game pieces on the board helping fulfill some bizarre cosmic duty that our simple human minds can't understand. An opposing take is that these portals are a type of subconscious divination. Like we are always subconsciously searching for ways to connect pathways and bring our deepest aims into reality.

Either way, being mindful of your inner and outer portals is a potent and valuable way to keep yourself aligned with your authentic path and prevent you from staying stuck in the story of who you think you have to be. The key is *trusting* your instincts and understanding how the opportunities that arise for you will almost always combine different aspects of yourself that you'd never thought to connect before. That's one of the fascinating things about these portals. Almost like a Zen poem, they connect two things you're good at or two things you're passionate about that aren't connected at all. The process unifies elements of who we are and creates powerful new forms of strength that we wouldn't have considered available.

> **Listen to what arises on your internal landscape. Be present, and don't ignore the opportunities you see appearing before you. They are showing up for a reason.**

Regardless if that's because it's fate or your subconscious mind seeking them, they are a path forward for you to realize your higher authentic self. Some might think it takes courage to let go of the story of who you are and redefine yourself. But it doesn't really. Because when you listen deeply and honestly observe what's happening inside of you, you will feel a sense of knowing. Knowing is different from confidence. Confidence is a mindset. It's thinking that you are prepared and capable of handling a situation. Knowing is a *feeling*. It is seeing the game for what it is and understanding that you can't fail because you are the one who's meant to be playing.

CHAPTER 18

FACING THE FUTURE WITH SELF-TRUST

Of all the practices, methods, and mindsets you can learn, the one that matters the most is learning to trust yourself. If you can learn to do that, you'll be able to deal with anything that comes your way. You won't have to rely on a preloaded method or a list of memorized quotes to help you through whatever you're dealing with. You'll feel comfortable in your own skin, be able to calmly work with any problem, improvise, and have the mental strength to keep moving forward whenever you face a challenge.

Of course, being able to live this way sounds great. But most of us struggle with self-belief and have a hard time trusting we can navigate life when the waters get choppy. That's understandable. Our paths are often filled with twists that throw us off our game and make us question our power, clarity, and self-belief. On top of that, no one teaches us how to be mentally self-reliant. Sure, we might be shown how to be *self-sufficient*—like making sure we can pay our bills and stay alive. But no one shows us how to emotionally and mentally deal with the unexpected problems, barriers, and pivots we all face.

That's because it can't be taught. And it definitely doesn't just happen on its own. You have to build it over time. That's what makes it work.

You accomplish something special by embracing challenges when they arise, using the tools you have learned to maintain a nonreactive and positive mindset, and staying open to shifting plans when needed. You prove to yourself how capable you are.

Through this process of facing challenges, being mentally flexible, and applying solutions, you craft a type of self-trust that feels like it's carved out of stone. When you feel overwhelmed, or the universe sabotages your plans, you can overcome and improve the situation by relying on your intuition and mental clarity. Each time you do this, it makes you stronger and gives you a track record of success to reflect on that bolsters the confidence you have going forward.

I'm sure you know people like this. They've put in the work and have a sturdy and clear presence about them. That's because they've been patient, consistent, and persistent over time and learned who they are in the process. The wisdom and calm that radiates from them communicates an unspoken virtue of humble self-belief that feels inspiring to be close to. You simply know that they know. You can see it in their eyes and feel the vibrations coming from their body.

A quote attributed to Arnold Schwarzenegger nails why building this feeling of self-trust is so powerful. Even though he's talking about our physical bodies in this quote, it also directly applies to our inner strength.

> A well-built physique is a symbol. It reflects you worked hard for it; no money can buy it. You cannot borrow it. You cannot inherit it. You cannot steal it. You cannot hold onto it without constant work. It shows discipline. It shows self-respect, it shows patience, work ethic, and passion. That is why I do what I do.

There's no "hack" that's going to help you trust yourself faster. There aren't 12 tips that will change your life overnight. The only real secret is that there are no secrets. You just have to start living as who you want to be. You have to know that life isn't going to be a succession of green lights.

> **You're going to face challenges. You will feel lost or like you don't have the confidence to keep going. But when those moments arise, you simply use what you've learned to shift your mindset, let go of negative thinking habits, and boldly move forward with curiosity, clarity, and a connection to the wisdom of your inner voice.**

The elements that help us cultivate this kind of strength are a mixture of self-trust, confidence, and knowing. Let's look at those three things separately so we can clearly understand how they help us tune in to our higher nature when combined.

- ***Self-trust*** is feeling comfortable that you can count on yourself. No matter the situation you face—good or bad—you know you will show up well. You won't avoid your problems and seek distractions. And you won't get short-sighted when you succeed because you always have the big picture in mind. You feel strongly that you won't fumble your good fortune and will always strive to be the best version of yourself that you can be, not only for you but for everyone around you.
- ***Confidence*** is feeling prepared to deal with any situation that may arise. You understand that life is full of moving parts. However, you can handle anything by working to become more self-aware,

mentally clear, and calm under pressure. You don't feel confident because you are overly sure of yourself. You feel that way because you are at ease in your body, have learned to flow with the bends of your path, and have a mindset that you can solve problems, be strong, and rise to the occasion when you must.

- ***Knowing*** is a feeling. It's being in touch with your intuition and letting it guide you from the inside out. Knowing is when you can *feel* what's going on, read between the lines in yourself and in life, and proceed with unwavering clarity that allows you to move forward without needing all the answers. When you *know,* you can feel which direction is right on your path. Then you can walk toward it with a flawlessness that cuts through space, time, and self-limitation.

For the rest of this chapter, we will look at key approaches to help you cultivate the strong sense of inner resilience we've been discussing. By keeping these points in the front of your mind, you'll find that a feeling of self-trust will start to solidify in your life from the inside out.

Things Will Go Well, Then They Won't, and That's Fine

Everyone wishes they could live a life without problems. For good reason too. One of the worst things is getting knocked out of our positive flow and having to regroup. When our path gets an unexpected twist, it derails our plans, drains our energy, and stresses us out. To make things worse, bad stuff always seems to happen at the worst possible moment. It's like the universe conspires to wait until we are already tired, stressed, and overscheduled, then hits us with a problem that makes our tension 10 times worse. If you can hang on to your sense of humor in moments like these, it's laughable how well, or should I say poorly timed, this stuff can feel.

However, the truth is that bad things in our lives don't happen at the worst possible times. They just happen. And they feel terribly timed because bad things are inherently disruptive. So no matter what's going on with us, when outside forces blow up our flow, it feels like the worst thing ever. Because of this, many of us worry that our groove will get whacked at the worst possible moment—especially when things are going well. Living like this creates anxiety that keeps us from getting in tune with our self-trust. If we're always feeling shaky, we can't feel strong.

How do we overcome this?

By confronting the truth about reality.

> **The fact is that life will *always* be a balance of joy and suffering. Things will go well. Then they won't. Then they will. It's just how life works. The key is recognizing that life is a balance of good and bad and that *how you engage with those moments* is what matters.**

Understanding that you'll run into bumps on the path is essential, because confronting that truth means you'll stop worrying about *when* things will go off track. You know life isn't perfect. So you use your mental strength to consciously work with whatever arises without it becoming a dramatic catastrophe.

Moving through life like this creates a conscious maturity that allows you to limit *needless* suffering. Knowing that life has ups and downs keeps you cool. It helps you enjoy the good things you experience without fearing they will be ruined by something going wrong. That's because you know when you have to deal with some challenges, you can keep your mindset positive, calmly handle them, and keep moving forward without getting knocked out of your flow.

Being Present with What's Small Creates Big Results

Life is complicated. There's so much to explore and so many options and possibilities, large and small. The problem is that because there's so much potential on the road ahead of us, it becomes too much to process. So we start to feel overwhelmed and end up shutting down rather than making a solid plan for how we will get to a higher level. On top of that, everyone on social media seeming to have it all figured out adds a lot of extra pressure. The nagging feeling that we need to "keep up" and "succeed" often results in a *downward* pressure that can depress our nervous system. Thinking this way makes us feel stuck, like nothing matters, and there aren't any real stakes in what we're doing with our lives.

The longer we believe this, the longer we drift, minimize ourselves, and bypass our emotions. This pulls us away from doing anything that will create meaning for us, and even worse, it makes us feel *ineffective.* Feeling like we can't influence our own paths strangles our ability to feel confident, which severely limits our ability to expand in any way that might be helpful.

Here's a good reality check: no one has it all figured out. Not you, me, your favorite musician, author, actor, podcaster, or entrepreneur.

Everyone is figuring it out as they go—even if it doesn't look that way from the outside. Understanding this is the key to building a resilient connection with your self-trust. You simply have to start moving forward and making the clearest choices you can so things can start happening for you.

Another truth people always get backward: You don't wait until your path is flourishing to make intentional choices. Your path starts flourishing *because* you began making clear choices in the first place.

Making intentional choices creates clarity, self-knowing, and inner strength. And you can start doing it from this moment forward. Being intentional isn't a lofty, fancy, or precious pursuit. It's not about coming up with a master plan that will take you from aimlessly drifting to being a billionaire in three years. It's much smaller than that—literally. Being intentional is about being *present* for the small moments in your life and constantly guiding them in a way that feels right.

Let's call what powers this your micro-intuition. Being purposeful about everything you do has massive compound effects on the big picture of life. How you speak, what you eat, who you are around, how you shift your mindset, how you practice self-care, how you approach your business, and much more all add up big time. In the beautiful pages of *The Book of Tea*, Okakura Kakuzō poetically shares why the traditional Japanese tea ceremony puts so much emphasis and ritualization on the small, seemingly meaningless, aspects of preparing a cup of tea. Doing so serves as a reminder that we often overlook the importance, beauty, and power of the small routines of our day. By applying intentional focus to them, we become present, grounded, and in closer touch with the essence of reality. As the saying goes, "How you do anything is how you do everything."

Greatness and self-connection are created slowly from the inside out. Start living with intention around everything you do. Stop shortchanging the power of your choices. *Be there* every step of the way. When you start living like this, you start using the power of your discernment to thoughtfully shape who you are in the present, which impacts who you will be in the future.

> **Remember that each small choice you make stacks up over time. Once you are more precise with what's small in your life, you will wake up one day and realize that tending to them is the only way to build something big.**

Do Less, but Do It Deeply

Nothing shaves down our self-trust like living on autopilot. If you can't hear yourself think or slow down enough to feel what you feel, you have no shot at knowing who you are. When we move too fast, we live in a constant state of reaction. This removes the possibility for us to think and act mindfully. If we aren't thinking mindfully, we are essentially living out the automations of our past conditioning. This leaves no space for us to hear our inner voice. The longer we go without hearing our inner voice, the fewer opportunities we have to build a connection to our self-trust through consciously navigating our experience.

Of course, it happens. We get caught in the waves of our lives while trying to hungrily pack in as much activity as we can. We become perpetually on the move. Living like this builds a habit of "touching" many things without deeply understanding or integrating them. Doing this causes the experience of almost everything in our lives to become fleeting and surface level. And as mentioned earlier, it disconnects us from the reflective wisdom of our inner voice.

Our brains constantly optimize their behavior, regardless of whether it's what we want. Human brains want to conserve biological energy. So if we do something often, they build in a sort of "default" neural path so we can perform our habit more easily. Spending enough time in a pattern of rapid living causes our neural pathways to rewire in an attempt to more effectively serve our surface-level engagement with reality. When that happens, we become *designed* to have short attention spans and be highly reactive.

This change doesn't just keep us from being present and able to deeply experience the richness that life has to offer. It begins to make us feel that a blurred, unfocused, and fidgety mind is *how things are*. The longer we live in this state of mind, the more we accept that surface-level self-awareness and shallow inner-knowing are all that are possible. We forget that a deeper, clearer, and more connected reality is simply waiting for us to remember that it exists.

Don't beat yourself up if this is your current habit. The truth is that *most* people are living this way. Technology makes it hard not to. Also, it's easy to change. It just takes a little consistency and intention. Essentially, you have to rewrite the script of your behavior to rewire the pathways of your mind.

There are endless ways you can program slow habits in your life. It's not so much *what* it is that you're doing. It's *how* you're doing it. For example, you might slow down one of your normal daily routines. If you stretch in the morning, put everything aside, and spend five minutes deeply, intentionally doing it rather than banging it out in 30 seconds. When you shower, don't hop in and ruminate over work drama or rehash old conversations in your head. Bring your mind closer to the present moment. Feel the indulgence, flow, and restorative nature of the water rolling across your body.

Whatever it is that you choose, slow it down.

> **Be intentional. Reconnect your mind to your experience and then release yourself to it. Do less. But do it deeply.**

Other broader ways you can reclaim your mental stillness include:

- Do a technology fast. No screens for more than 10 minutes a day, for one week, except ones you must use during work hours.
- Practice meditation every day. Spend 20 minutes a day sitting quietly and focusing on your breathing.
- Take a daily walk without headphones. Instead of pumping more information into your head, connect with the sounds of the world.
- Spend an extra long time making a delicious meal without listening to a podcast or music. Enjoy the spaciousness of silence and being.

What's interesting is that even when you think you're good at self-connecting and slowing down, you can easily discover that you have much more room to go. I'm from Austin, Texas, and in the last few years we've had a hard time managing our power grid. Winter storms, excessive heat, or heavy rains have occasionally knocked out power for huge chunks of the city. It happened again a few months before I started writing this book. No matter how well I think I remember what it feels like to spend several days in silence with minimal digital devices, I'm always surprised at how wild the difference is when I do.

Having the mental space to hear your own voice, come back into the present, and simply "be" dramatically clarifies your thinking. Now, you don't need a thunderstorm to knock out your power to make it happen. Thoughtfully build spaces in your life where you can slow down, step out of the perpetual state of doing, and hear your inner voice. Doing this will strengthen your connection to your intuition. By building that connection, you'll be able to guide yourself from that deep place during the entire course of your day—growing self-trust, confidence, and a potent form of knowing.

Failure Is a Path to Greater Things If You're Open

We go through life expecting things to work out exactly how we want them to. Even though we *know* the universe doesn't operate that way, we can't help but do it anyway. So when our plans don't work out—or simply change—we generally react, get tense, and feel deflated, bummed, and disconnected from our self-trust.

I'm sure you know that feeling of deep existential disappointment. We all do. And it isn't pleasant. Believe it or not, knowing this feeling is a *good thing*. I know. That doesn't really make sense. But it's true.

> **Having a strong reaction to your plans not working out means that you're still trying, and you still believe. It means you are striving to level up your life and improve your relationships, opportunities, and strength of self. It means that *your spirit is* still alive, and you are still swirling with a hunger to reach higher levels of your personal evolution.**

That's crucial. Because as long as you still have an ember, you can always figure out a way to build a raging fire.

It took a lot of repetition in my life (things not working out for me over and over) before I started applying my mindful lens to tough moments. Even though I'd practiced mindfulness for years, when something I had high hopes for didn't pan out, I would still feel like I got dumped into an emotional landfill. Thankfully, my inner practices developed, and my mindful awareness became more sturdy. Then these letdowns stopped fazing me as much. This allowed me to look at them with a larger perspective. When I started doing that, I had a breakthrough that serves me to this day.

I realized that when things didn't work out how I wanted, it forced me to *think in new ways* that wouldn't have been possible without that big letdown. Every single time, the shift in thinking, even though it was rough in the short term, led to something bigger, better, and more fruitful than what I initially aimed for. It was *because* of something not working out that I had other ideas that were more powerful. The key was that instead of getting pulled into the mental drama of the moment, I was calm, thoughtful, and looked at *what was possible* rather than what wasn't.

As you continue working to lift up your life, empower your authentic self, and achieve the greatness you desire, remember that your expectations are simply that: what you expect to happen. Knowing what you *expect* to happen isn't what *will* happen is quite stabilizing. And really, who would want everything to work out how they expect it to? How boring would that be? It's the push and pull of our path that creates growth. The growing pains stop once we learn how to use the fresh creative thoughts that are triggered by our plans changing to our advantage.

Watch your mind when you are living in expectation mode and your plans are forcibly changed. Stay calm, open, and curious. Don't grasp the outcome you thought you wanted. Notice that your mind will respond to the changing situation with a plethora of alternate possibilities. Then, use your intuition to feel which one is right, and use your mental clarity to formulate a superior iteration of your plan. Once you do this, you'll be stunned at how much better things are going than you'd hoped. Working with change in this way builds a deep self-connection to your ability to trust your judgment and creatively evolve your goals.

In time, you'll find that what you face in life aren't problems but opportunity pathways to greater things.

Listen to Your Inner Voice, Even When It Comes from a Stranger's Mouth

At the end of the day, all you have to guide you in this life is your inner voice. Friends, family members, mentors, and co-workers can offer valuable feedback. But no matter how well someone knows you, they still don't know you better than you do. People are infinite wells of thoughts, emotions, and meaning. At best, we can share 10 percent of who we are, what we think, and how we feel through language. Now, that's just a rough guess of a percentage, as measuring something like that would be quite difficult. The point is that so much of who we are is completely unknown and unknowable to other people. Ninety percent of your whole being—your insights, wisdom, and knowing—is private. You are the only one who has access.

Deep and complex layers of thoughts, feelings, and forces live inside you, constantly changing, evolving, and becoming richer. As these pieces of Self swirl around and unify within you, they create a beautiful resonant sound. That sound is the tone of your consciousness. It's all the pieces of you coming together, working with existence in a feedback loop as you navigate the story of your life. If you listen closely, you can hear a voice within that tone of mind.

> **Beyond the random thought fragments that move across the stage of your awareness, you can hear an inner voice that feels like it has existed since the beginning of time. It's deep, true, and firm.**

Regardless of what's happening in life, the voice is always steady, reliable, and clear when it speaks. It can't be overwhelmed. It isn't indecisive. It can't be quiet. It knows. This voice is your intuition—the part of you that always has an answer and has no cause for reasoning.

Maybe you think of it in a slightly different metaphor, but I have no doubt you know what I'm talking about. Your inner voice is that razor-sharp gut feeling you have about everything. Beneath the tension of the intellect, it's always there, urging you to move in a clear direction. The problem is that we love fighting with the inner voice that's trying to help us. We do this because the flow of our consciousness goes intuition > emotion > intellect. We start with a clear intuition of what to do, feel a way about it, then try to apply logic to it. Doing this makes us get in our own way. We complicate and misdirect what we know is true by trying to retrofit it to an existing narrative that we're attached to.

However, if you can learn to listen to that inner voice without mutating its message, you will excel in every area of your life more than you can imagine. We spend so much time fighting with ourselves, caught in a web of our emotions and logic, that we use most of our energy processing rather than executing. In *Essays in Zen Buddhism,* the invaluable scholar D. T. Suzuki offered the notion that enlightenment is getting out of your own way so the fullness of what you are can come through. Indeed, an enlightened state of mind is living from the force of your intuitive, gut-level wisdom while simply turning your intellect into the sail of a boat that helps navigate your experience on behalf of your deeper knowing. Living in this state gives you lightning-fast decision-making skills, allows you to "ride the wind," and fosters a kind of self-trust that's rooted *beneath* the foundation of where your self-limiting thoughts live.

> **Intuitive power is the result of getting your conscious and subconscious minds to work together more fluidly.**

This is one of the reasons people who meditate experience higher levels of mental clarity, calm, and self-awareness. In my experience, meditation thins the theoretical membrane that separates our conscious and subconscious minds. With that barrier clear, our total mind becomes more self-integrated, which means that we can spend less time fighting with ourselves about what we *should* be doing and more time doing what we feel we are *meant* to do.

Now before we wrap things up, let's have some fun. I want to leave you with, well, let's call it a question and an answer wrapped into one. As you power forward in your life, trusting yourself and listening to your inner voice, you will start to notice something strange. Something uncanny. Maybe something that's magical. Honestly, I'm not even sure what it is or what to call it. After experiencing it countless times, I think the fact that I have no idea *why* it happens is exactly why it works.

Every now and then, I'll get into a flow of listening to my intuition *without* prejudice. And sure, I like to think I do that all the time, but honestly, there's always a little critical voice in my mind sizing everything up. But sometimes that voice steps out for a coffee break and things get magical. I start hearing the guiding inner voice and it takes over. It's all I can hear, and the more I listen, the more *energy* it gives me. I don't judge it. I just open up and let it come through.

When that happens, I start noticing wild stuff. It's like the inner message I'm receiving starts showing up everywhere. One of my favorite examples of this happened before I wrote my first book, *Now Is the Way*. I'd wanted to write a book for some time, but not everything was in place yet. Then one day I started feeling an intuitive signal that the time had come. The *day* I had that thought, I was having lunch with a friend. The people at the table next to us were talking and one of them said, "You should write a book" to their friend. As I was driving, I saw a billboard for a vacation company that said, "BOOK TODAY." On the same ride home, I was listening to a podcast, and Stephen King's book *On Writing* happened to be recommended for budding writers. Then, later that afternoon—in all honesty—I got an e-mail from a literary agent asking if I had considered writing a book.

When I get deeply connected to my intuitive voice and allow my mental antenna to be sensitive, it's like a cosmic message follows me around. I see it in strange places, fragments of related sentences come out of strangers' mouths, and uncanny things start happening. It's like the universe is pushing the signs through every possible channel, hoping that I'm not too hung up on myself to see them. There's an intoxicating feeling that comes with this too. It's like everything is tuned so perfectly that it creates a spectacular energetic harmony. Every time this has happened, and I've been open enough to listen, it's led to something life-changing.

Now, on one hand, this phenomenon makes a lot of sense. If you're thinking about something, it's going to be front of mind, so you'll start to see patterns that represent that. On the other hand, it doesn't make any sense whatsoever. I mean, "BOOK TODAY." C'mon. How could something that blatant and funny not have at least a little magic dust flowing off it. That's why a few paragraphs back I said this was an answer and a question rolled into one.

The answer is that this strange magic will guide you to incredible places if you're willing to listen. The question, of course, is what in the world is guiding the forces that are guiding you?

I have no idea. But what I do know is that, above everything else, please, I beg you, have fun with your future.

> **Allow yourself to be curious. Go in odd directions. Do things *your* way. Don't let other people's baggage keep you from experiencing some magic of your own.**

Listen to your intuitive voice. Explore what's possible in your life. Surprise yourself. Keep trusting and listening to the energy inside of you. When you're open and you start tuning in to something, watch for your own signs following you around. Then play with them. See what happens when you follow through on those seismic waves of knowing that rise from deep within you.

You might just learn this life is larger and stranger than any of us can imagine. You might just discover that there are forces inside *and* outside of you that are trying to guide you to your perfect place in the universe. You might hear your future come out of a stranger's mouth. And when you do, I only ask that you do one thing.

Listen.

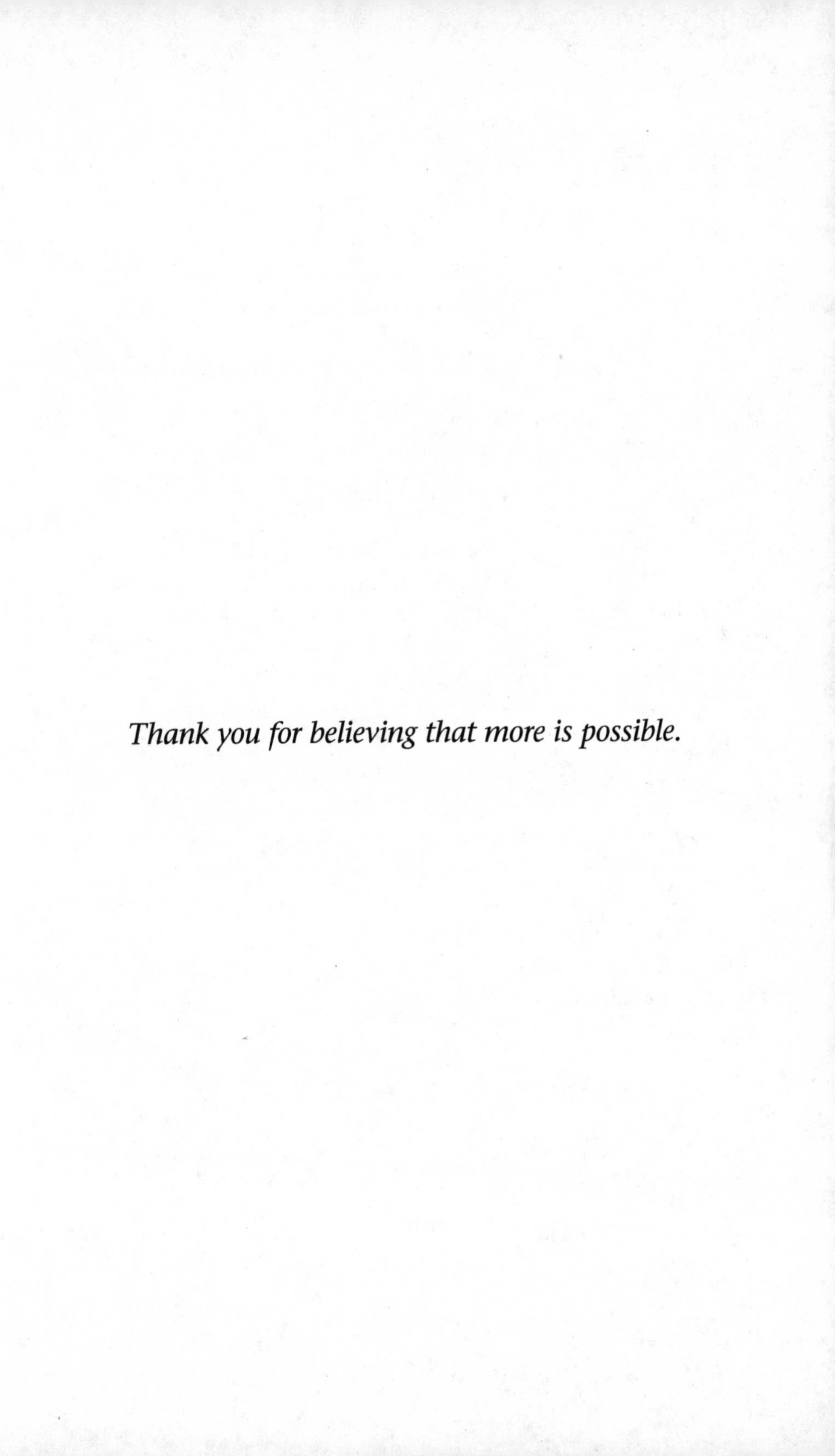

Thank you for believing that more is possible.

ABOUT THE AUTHOR

Cory Allen is a wave of awareness that is currently floating in the middle of infinity. More specifically, he is an author, podcaster, influencer, and music producer. Allen writes daily motivational thoughts on mental clarity for his large Instagram following, reaching over a million people a week, and has been featured in *The New York Times*. He lives in Austin, TX, with his brilliant wife Meredith and luscious golden retriever Bowie.

Hay House Titles of Related Interest

YOU CAN HEAL YOUR LIFE, the movie,
starring Louise Hay & Friends
(available as an online streaming video)
www.hayhouse.com/louise-movie

THE SHIFT, the movie,
starring Dr. Wayne W. Dyer
(available as an online streaming video)
www.hayhouse.com/the-shift-movie

***

GOOD VIBES, GOOD LIFE: How Self-Love Is the Key to Unlocking Your Greatness, by Vex King

SH#T YOUR EGO SAYS: Strategies to Overthrow Your Ego and Become the Hero of Your Story, by James McCrae

LETTING GO: The Pathway of Surrender, by David R. Hawkins, M.D., Ph.D.

All of the above are available at your local bookstore, or may be ordered by contacting Hay House (see next page).

***

We hope you enjoyed this Hay House book. If you'd like to receive our online catalog featuring additional information on Hay House books and products, or if you'd like to find out more about the Hay Foundation, please contact:

Hay House LLC, P.O. Box 5100, Carlsbad, CA 92018-5100
(760) 431-7695 or (800) 654-5126
www.hayhouse.com® • www.hayfoundation.org

Published in Australia by:
Hay House Australia Publishing Pty Ltd
18/36 Ralph St., Alexandria NSW 2015
Phone: +61 (02) 9669 4299
www.hayhouse.com.au

Published in the United Kingdom by:
Hay House UK Ltd
The Sixth Floor, Watson House,
54 Baker Street, London W1U 7BU
Phone: +44 (0) 203 927 7290
www.hayhouse.co.uk

Published in India by:
Hay House Publishers (India) Pvt Ltd
Muskaan Complex, Plot No. 3,
B-2, Vasant Kunj, New Delhi 110 070
Phone: +91 11 41761620
www.hayhouse.co.in